MARIACHI

MARIACHI

Patricia Greathouse

GIBBS SMITH
TO ENRICH AND INSPIRE HUMANKIND
Salt Lake City | Charleston | Santa Fe | Santa Barbara

First Edition
13 12 11 10 09   5 4 3 2 1

Text © 2009 Patricia Greathouse
Photography © 2009 as noted

Title page: Joel Rivera of Mariachi Corazón del Desierto, Deming,
New Mexico. photo © 2009 Christopher Barnes
Above facing: photo © 2009 Patricia Greathouse.
Below facing: photo © 2009 Madeleine de Sinety.

Published by

Gibbs Smith

P.O. Box 667

Layton, Utah 84041

1.800.835.4993 orders

www.gibbs-smith.com

Designed and produced by Kurt Wahlner
Printed and bound in China
Gibbs Smith books are printed on either recycled, 100% post-
consumer waste, FSC-certified papers or on paper produced from
a 100% certified sustainable forest/controlled wood source.

Library of Congress Cataloging-in-Publication Data

Greathouse, Patricia.
  Mariachi / Patricia Greathouse. — 1st ed.
     p. cm.
  ISBN-13: 978-1-4236-0281-1
  ISBN-10: 1-4236-0281-1
  1. Mariachi—History and criticism. 2. Popular music—Mexico—
History and criticism. 3. Folk dance music—Mexico—History and
criticism. I. Title.
  ML3485.G74 2009
  781.64089'6872—dc22
               2008040744

To my husband
and partner,
Chris, whose
generosity,
enthusiasm,
and hard
work make
everything
possible

CONTENTS

FOREWORD

Why do mariachi ensembles exist all over the world—ensembles that perform Mexico's national music in South America, the United States, the Dominican Republic, Canada, Japan, Croatia, Holland, and Rome? The proverbial answer, "Music is the universal language," could be cited, but why mariachi music? What is the worldwide attraction to mariachi—the music, the history, the characters, the lore? In the last forty to fifty years there has been an increase in interest, ranging from the incidental to serious academic research to a great transcultural recognition and a desire to somehow be involved in Mexico's most popular folk music.

I first noticed Patricia Greathouse and her husband, Chris Barnes, at the Las Cruces International Mariachi Conference, purposefully making their way among members of Mariachi Cobre and various other attendees. She finally introduced herself to me and told me what she was doing and asked me for an interview. I gladly accepted, and one evening, after a long day of activities, we sat and talked. Patricia gave me the opportunity to recount the early days of the first *mariachi juvenil* (youth mariachi) in the United States in 1964—Los Changuitos Feos—and how Mariachi

Randy Carrillo. Photo © 2009 Christopher Barnes.

Cobre was born from this then-unique ensemble in 1971. Different geographical areas of the United States had their mariachi genesis in their own time and in their unique way, and I feel fortunate to have had mine in Tucson, Arizona, first with Los Changuitos Feos, and then the great experience with my family and friends in Mariachi Cobre.

This gem of a book offers a great blend of historical fact, storytelling, and opinion about a musical form that began as a provincial pastime but has grown to establish itself around the world. My personal involvement with Patricia and her book has given me a new appreciation for the writers who chronicle the cultural events of this genre for the benefit and pleasure of us all. Patricia's book brings the musical, social, economic, educational, and historical impact of mariachi into focus.

Keep writing and reading!

Randy Carrillo
Founder/Director, Mariachi Cobre
Orlando, Florida

Stephen Carrillo, Mariachi Cobre's musical director. Photo © 2009 Christopher Barnes.

PREFACE

I grew up as a middle-class Anglo in Las Cruces, New Mexico. My family, westerners for many generations, lived side by side with the descendents of the Mexicans who originally owned the land. My early life was full of Mexican music; it floated on the air we breathed. Spanish was often more common than English; I'm still enchanted by its cadence. In my friends' homes, I experienced a first-hand glimpse of the culture, attending baptismal parties, weddings, and feast days. I couldn't get enough, but I was on the outside. My fair hair and blue eyes always gave me away.

When I went to school in Mexico City one summer, I expected to see adobe houses, saguaro cactuses, donkeys, and sleepy sombreroed Mexicans napping in the shade. Landing at the airport and taxiing through Mexico City, my eyes took in the chaos and struggle of the megalopolis. That summer began my true education in the complexity of Mexican culture and my lifelong love of mariachi music. Although I had grown up with it, I had never understood how clearly mariachi music tells of the intensity and pathos of Mexican life. The music drove its way into my heart, commanding my attention in a way I had never experienced.

Many years later, a fellow violinist from the Santa Fe Community Orchestra invited me to try out with her group, Mariachi Azteca. I was enchanted from the first rehearsal. The music was challenging; the lead singer, Eddie Hernández, was amazing. Wearing the traje, we were gods. I, at last, had an entry into the Mexican culture.

I feel full of the spirit of Mexico when I play mariachi music. The music speaks to my soul. After my father died, nothing moved me as much as Juan Gabriel's "Amor Eterno." I had to leave the room or risk tears staining my violin. Perhaps that is the key to this music—it penetrates to the deepest corners of our hearts, regardless of where we come from.

Patricia Greathouse

ACKNOWLEDGMENTS

Many thanks for Ellen Kleiner, who came up with the idea for this book, to Gibbs Smith, who believed in the vision, and to my editor, Leslie Stitt, for being so cheerful, helpful, and supportive.

My deepest gratitude and thanks go to Sherry James, who read, edited, and gave invaluable feedback on both my writing and on Spanish translations.

The number of mariachis I spoke to is too large to list, so please forgive me if I have failed to thank you; your contribution is here. I have tried to identify and obtain all the permissions necessary; if I have failed, please accept my apologies.

For me, the greatest thrill was being able to talk to the mariachi legends—Miguel Martínez, Jesús Rodríguez de Híjar, Rigoberto Alfaro, and Heriberto Molina—who, although mariachi titans, are humble and sincere.

The members of Mariachi Cobre were exceedingly generous. Many thanks to Randy and Stephen Carrillo. Antonio Hernández and Hector and Carlos Gama were instrumental in helping me understand the difference in the lives of mariachis in the United States and Mexico, as well as the importance of good musicianship as opposed to "mariachi style."

José Hernández made time for an interview while he was directing a conference, an unbelievable act of kindness.

To Mariachi Tenampa, long-time friends and compadres, many thanks for your help.

In Mexico, Mariachi Sol de América of Guadalajara took me in and treated me like a sister. Armando Cervantes Tinoco has continued to answer questions and to be a wonderful resource. Antonio Covarrubias came to my Mexico City hotel with back issues of his magazine *El Mariachi Sueno,* CDs, and pictures. He impressed me deeply with the hardship professional mariachis face in Mexico.

I am indebted to Mariachi Vargas, especially Pepe Martínez and Federico Torres, who gave me interviews and invited me along on a venue, allowing me an inside view of the most venerable mariachi in the world. It was a dream come true.

The women mariachis I spoke to were inspiring, helpful and gracious, telling me their stories when they were so busy balancing their lives that they could hardly find time to speak.

Thank you to Mariachi Azteca for years of music making.

Jesús Jaúregui, the foremost Mexican scholar of mariachi, gave me important and generous support, explaining the development of mariachi, giving me his writing, and making himself available to me at a time when he was busy trying to get his own book into print. His American counterpart, Jonathan Clark, the top American expert on mariachi, was also incredibly generous, correcting text, giving me a long interview, and helping me fill in gaps in my knowledge.

Finally, thank you to my family and friends, who were patient and never complained when I turned them down to work on the book.

WHAT IS MARIACHI?

The violins soar and weep, the trumpets blare and caress, the armonía section beats a tight and intricate rhythm. The dazzling uniforms flash with every movement. The singer holds every heart in her hands. Emotions rise, faces glow, tears fall. The music is at once so exotic, so passionate, that it could come only from that mix of cultures that is Mexico. ¡Que viva mariachi!

TRADITIONAL MARIACHI

Veteran mariachi on Plaza Garibaldi, Mexico City. Photo © 2009 Madeleine de Sinety. BELOW: Competitors at the national charrería, Lagos de Moreno, Jalisco, Mexico. Photo © 2009 Madeleine de Sinety.

An ethnomusicologist once told me that a complete, exhaustive study of traditional mariachi would fill ten large volumes. Each village is its own unique study. Similar to American Appalachian music, untrained traditional mariachis flavor and add, cut and shape. It is unique and intense music that reflects its birthplace. It sprang from European roots, came alive with African beats, and thrived in the soil of the indigenous New World. As Appalachian music spawned bluegrass, traditional mariachi begot a virtuosic commercial form: modern mariachi music.

Wars and poverty forced populations to move to the cities, and as formerly rural mariachis relocated to Mexico City, their music changed. No longer an integral part of community celebrations, mariachi evolved to be an urban expression of traditional roots. Whether played in the street, in the recording studio, or on the film stage, it became a standardized and homogenized commodity, the result of mixing regional styles, professional arrangements, and trained musicians.

Compared to the modern mariachi, traditional rural mariachis are a rarity—the music is not commercially viable, and it is uninteresting to generations who have grown up with electronic music. Remote villages in Spanish colonial areas of the United States (like the mountains of northern New Mexico) still harbor some remnants of the tradition. Ethnomusicologists and other scholars are interested in traditional mariachi as a pure cultural expression. They see it as worthy of preservation, and some go so far as to play authentic music in the rough manner of untrained musicians, wearing coarse homespun manta for performances. Meanwhile, the carriers of the culture, musicians who still remember the old music, are dying out.

Mariachi Sol de Mexico's trademark suede traje and matching boots.
Photo © 2009 Patricia Greathouse.

MODERN MARIACHI

Modern mariachi is the music everyone has heard on the radio, at parties, and at community celebrations. Mariachis on the street and on the stage, whether in Mexico, Los Angeles, or Santa Fe, are modern mariachis. It is a distinct form and it is the focus of this book.

The word "mariachi" has several related meanings. First, it refers to a person who plays mariachi music. A name also used in Mexico for a mariachi musician is *mariachero* (male) or *mariachera* (female). The second meaning of "mariachi" refers to the whole group. The third meaning of the word denotes the particular style of music: mariachi music. Some mariachis take issue with this usage, saying that there is no such thing as "mariachi music." They say that it is "la música mexicana"; however, the phrase "mariachi music" is used commonly in English. Some also consider "mariachi band" to be an improper name for a mariachi group. For our purposes, a mariachi plays mariachi music in a mariachi group. A singer who isn't a regular member of a group is a guest soloist, not a mariachi, even though he or she is wearing a *traje de charro*. All mariachis play instruments, and all mariachis sing, at least on the choruses. In the very best mariachis, all the group members are excellent singers, capable of taking center stage and delivering an outstanding version of a song.

No one knows exactly where the word "mariachi" comes from, but the best guess is that it originated with the indigenous Coca people of western Mexico. Many Mexicans believe that it came from the French word for marriage, *mariage,* a mistake promulgated by Alfonso Reyes, a well-respected Mexican linguist, whose book *Nuestra Lengua (Our Language)* was distributed in Mexican schools in 1959. The idea has become fixed in the

A true charro at the International Charrería competition in Lagos de Moreno, Jalisco, Mexico, 2007. Photo © 2009 Jasper Schriber.

Young charros in Lagos de Moreno, Jalisco. Photo © 2009 Patricia Greathouse.

public consciousness, although there are written records of its use long before the French Intervention. In 1852, a Mexican priest from the small town of Rosamorada, Mexico, named Cosme Santa Anna wrote to his archbishop, using the word *mariache* and complaining of the unholy noise that musicians and dancers were making during *Semana Santa* (Holy Week). Since the French Intervention didn't begin until 1864, the theory of the French origin of the word seems doubtful.

The origins of mariachi music itself have long been debated, with proud proponents striving to declare their town the true birthplace. There is evidence that traditional mariachi developed in western Mexico, flowering in different places at about the same time. The states of Jalisco, Michoacán, Aguascalientes, Nayarit, Durango, Zacatecas, Guanajuato, Colima, and Sinaloa are all—to a greater or lesser degree—cradles of mariachi. Although traditional mariachi developed in all those places, Mexico City was the true birthplace of modern mariachi, the music that is known around the world.

THE MARIACHI UNIFORM

As part of creating a national Mexican identity, President Abelardo Rodríguez declared *charrería* (Mexican rodeo) the national sport in 1930. Proud traditional *charros*, gentlemen cowboys, still cherish the tradition, holding charrerías, or competitions, where they dress in the *traje de charro* and show off their beautiful, well-trained horses. Starting at an early age, both males and females participate in charrería, preserving the ranch culture of western Mexico.

The *traje de charro de gala* (called a "traje" for short) today typifies mariachi dress. Adapted from the outfit worn by rich charros, it gave poor musicians a more elegant and refined appearance. Charros didn't take kindly to mariachis copying their dress, and more than one distinguished gentleman has been offended by being mistaken for a mariachi.

For mariachis, however, switching to the traje de charro was an exterior sign of moving up in status. The transition from the country to the city and employment in the entertainment media required a new image. The charro's traje, individualistic and fit for riding a horse, underwent design changes by the mariachis that made it totally impractical for anything but playing music. In matching outfits in a rainbow of colors, today's mariachis flaunt stylishness and flash, and a group is immediately identifiable by its matching colors.

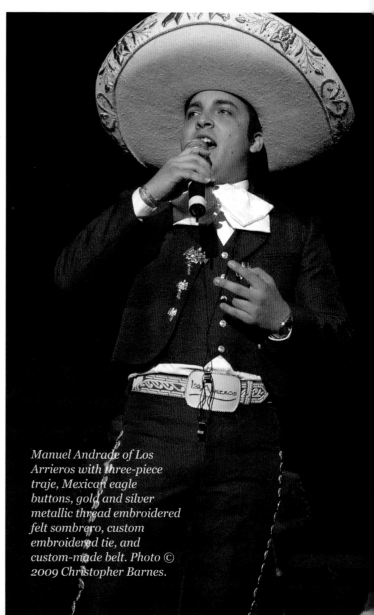

Manuel Andrade of Los Arrieros with three-piece traje, Mexican eagle buttons, gold and silver metallic thread embroidered felt sombrero, custom embroidered tie, and custom-made belt. Photo © 2009 Christopher Barnes.

The Libertad market in Guadalajara is a treasure trove of mariachi and folkloric apparel. Photo © 2009 Patricia Greathouse.

The cost of a simple traje starts at around a hundred dollars for a factory-made suit and rises to thousands for a tailor-made three-piece suede or chamois suit with hand embroidery and real silver botonadura (flashy buttons that decorate pants and jackets). Mini-skirts, hot pants, and bell bottoms all were briefly in vogue, but faded out with mullets and sideburns.

The soft, self-tied *moño* (necktie) of the charro and early mariachis now comes made-to-order in solid colors or embroidered. Silver and gold colored botonadura are made for the mariachi from die-cast metal instead of the charros' coin silver. Boots that were originally made to fit in a stirrup are now fashioned with flat heels for long hours of standing, dyed in hues to match trajes, and zippered for a tight fit.

The hats—ranging from a simple *sombrero de pata de trigo* (woven wheat-straw hat) to rabbit felt to sequin-embroidered—are all adapted from traditional Jaliscan charro styles.

The fine belts worn by mariachis are often custom embroidered with a group's name in maguey fiber. Cheaper, coarser styles imitate with cotton thread and larger stitches.

In Guadalajara, an entire street near the Libertad market caters to charros and mariachis and provides everything from less expensive off-the-rack charro costumes to the finest handmade suede traje de charro. Online companies sell mariachi and folkloric outfits at reasonable prices, reaping the benefits of the educational movement in the United States.

HISTORY OF MARIACHI MUSIC

Mexicans love music.

Everything from intimate moments to public fiestas has its own sound track. Before the arrival of the Spaniards in the New World, music, singing, and dancing were a prominent part of social and religious life. Indigenous rulers and priests sponsored community rituals in public plazas accompanied by well-prepared musicians. (In fact, a mistake in a performance could lead to execution.) The same tradition, minus the perfection and the penalty, was common in Spain and continues to this day in every part of Mexico.

Rural Mexican music undoubtedly grew out of these Mesoamerican and European roots, with African traditions mixed in. Like the mestizo people of the country, it is uniquely Mexican. Full of rhythm, passion, and stories, animistic and primal, it was the source from which sprang modern mariachi music.

Sadly, there was little written during the conquest about the music of the indigenous peoples of Mexico; most conquistadores considered the natives obstacles to overcome, not human beings with a culture of supreme interest. Neither is much known about the music of west Africa, or even of the music of the conquering Spanish. There is much conjecture about origins of Mexican folkloric music, but the heritage must be traced backward and involves guesswork. Until very recently, there was little interest or curiosity concerning the roots of popular music in Mexico.

INDIGENOUS MUSIC MAKING

We owe almost everything we know about the culture of preconquest and early colonial times in Mexico to a few men. The primary historians of the period were Bernardino de Sahagún, a

Mariachis onstage, Mexico City. Photo © 2009 Madeleine de Sinety. BELOW: Mariachi Mexico de Pepe Villa. Private collection of Patricia Greathouse.

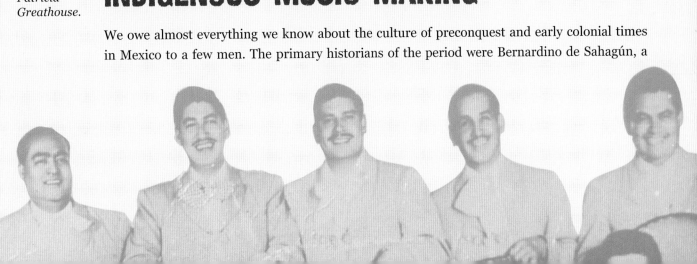

Franciscan missionary who recorded everything he learned from the *Nahua* (Aztecs) he ministered to; Diego Durán, Dominican chronicler with a lively interest in the native population; and Bernal Díaz, a conquistador who wrote an eyewitness account.

The instruments of preconquest Mexicans that have survived are the percussive instruments still used in the music of Latin America—drums, rattles, and scrapers—and primitive wind instruments—flutes, clay trumpets, and conch shell horns.

AFRICAN INFLUENCES

After a huge number of indigenous laborers died from disease and mistreatment, the Spanish bought Africans from Portuguese slavers to work their mines and sugarcane fields. Although the Spanish rulers had given their conquistadores clear instructions for the treatment of native people of the Americas, there were ways to get around them. According to decree, the natives would be Christianized, and, as fellow believers, should not be enslaved. However, those who resisted or reverted to their original practices might be used as slave labor. Cortéz managed to baptize members of many tribes, as instructed, but failed to give them Christian training. The newly converted continued with their old rites and religious practices. In the jaundiced eyes of the conquering Spaniards, who needed free labor, they had reverted to paganism. Natives became the property of mine owners and hacienda owners, who worked them without mercy. Some experts posit that as much as 85 percent of the population of Mexico today is descended from Mexican and African slaves. In fact, some experts think that there were more Africans in Mexico than there were Spaniards in the 1600s.

Africans were sturdier and somehow better able to deal with the set of physical challenges—European diseases in particular—that New World servitude presented. As many as six thousand Africans arrived at the port of Veracruz on slave ships during the early colonial period, and with them came the rhythms and musical traditions of western Africa. These slaves became an important part of the Mexican *mestizaje* (mix of peoples) that created the population from which regional Mexican music forms grew.

As a cultural group, they also had a large role in musical entertainment venues in the large cities. They taught music and dancing and got in trouble with the Inquisition for profane dances. Their songs were candid in their expression of antagonism for the Spanish, and they no doubt influenced the freedom with which later song lyrics were written.

THE SPANISH CONTRIBUTION

European music came on the boats with the Spanish invasion of Mexico in 1519. Cortéz's party included musicians who entertained the troops, singing and playing the harp and Spanish vihuela. As the army made its way toward Tenochtitlán, capital of the notoriously fierce and wealthy Nahua empire, the musicians fascinated natives along the way. Many of these joined the march against the tyrannical Nahua, to whom they had been paying tribute. Franciscan missionaries, too, found music to be a strong draw when winning souls. Spanish festivals and saints' days mixed with indigenous ceremonies, quickly becoming an integral part of life in New Spain and occasions for great celebration.

Not surprisingly, indigenous people readily adapted to a new approach to making music. Priests in Mexico City educated their students in counterpoint and European conventions, producing church musicians and composers. Manuel de Zumaya, a mestizo, became Mexico City chapel master in 1715. His compositions ranged in style from Renaissance to high baroque, and he wrote memorable masses and an opera in Italian.

Upper-class Mexicans loved Italian opera, and the *bel canto* singing technique has influenced the sound of the best contemporary mariachi singers.

THE ROOTS OF MARIACHI MUSIC

The beginnings of mariachi music are obscure. It seems to have sprung in the most natural way from the mountains, plains, and valleys of western Mexico. Tracing its early growth and transmission is like trying to track the path of a mycelium that grows underground. The gradual emergence of the genre happened while no one was looking.

Provincial mariacheros were villagers who made their living in simple ways. They took their status as musicians very seriously, often traveling long distances to play where they were needed. They sometimes slept on the ground after playing day and night for fiestas and saints' days. Some indigenous mariachis took vows of celibacy in order to be pure enough to receive the gift of music from the gods. Far-off gatherings were good places to meet fellow musicians, and they returned home with new tunes, learned by ear. In this way, tunes passed from person to person and village to village, acquiring distinct regional and individual flavors. Provincial musicians wore their everyday clothes and, depending on their subregion, used some combination of violin, guitar, guitars de golpe, vihuela, harp, and guitarrón. Occasionally groups included wind instruments such as the clarinet, saxophone, or cornet.

Traditional mariachi music developed as part of mestizo culture but was also adopted by indigenous communities. Huichol (or Wixáritari) mariachis in native dress can be seen playing on the streets around the Parián in Guadalajara from time to time. Many rural dwellers are anxious to move away from their primitive rural lifestyle and—thanks to technology— recorded music, electric

Huichol mariachis perform on a street in Tlaquepaque, Mexico. Photo credit © 2009 Patricia Greathouse.

guitars, and pop music are popular. In one tiny village we visited in Nayarit, musicians played the opening segment of a Bee Gees tune from *Saturday Night Fever* for hours, their electric guitar and amplifiers hooked up to a tiny generator in a woven stick shack.

1890 TO 1910

Mariachi Vargas (page 91) was founded in Tecalitlán, Jalisco, in 1898.

Perhaps the first time a mariachi from Jalisco played in Mexico City was Cuarteto Coculense de Justo Villa's performance for Porfirio Díaz's onomástico (saint's day) party in 1905. The audience loved the sound and rhythm of the sones, corridos, and jarabes the group played. They made recordings in 1907, playing sones Cocula style in strict $\frac{6}{8}$ time rather than the alternating $\frac{6}{8}$ to $\frac{3}{4}$ style that has come to be the standard.

Elihu Root, the Secretary of State of the United States, visited Mexico in 1908, and two mariachi groups dressed in traje de charro united under the name Orquesta Mariachi to play for his reception. The group was twice the size of a traditional mariachi—seven pieces instead of three to five.

1910 TO 1920

Between 1910 and 1920, the revolution swept Mexico, raging from the northern border to the southern part of the country. Battles destroyed homes and farms and caused countless civilian deaths. Whole villages were wiped out, and by some estimates, half the population of western Mexico was displaced. The diaspora fled to Mexico City and Guadalajara and to the United States. Cities were swollen with rural agrarian poor, who became the new urban poor.

Army regiments on both sides included musical groups, and armed revolutionary mariachi-soldiers played corridos that spread the news and told stories of the heroes of the revolution like Pancho Villa and La Adelita.

1920 TO 1930

Mariachi music became established in Mexico City during the '20s and '30s as regional groups poured into the capital under the patronage of politicians, the military, and the president. Unfortunately, mariachis still faced many hardships and often found it hard to earn a living.

Mexico changed a great deal during the 1920s as a result of revolution and subsequent land reform. Large landholdings were divided and redistributed, and egalitarian ideals were taking hold. Respect for indigenous peoples and pride in the country's rural roots joined the

spirit of nationalism and *patria* (country), while leaders were faced with uniting a country of diverse geographical and cultural regions.

In 1924, Secretary of Education José Vasconcelos proclaimed the *jarabe tapatío,* from the state of Jalisco, to be Mexico's national dance. During ballerina Anna Pavlova's tour of Mexico, she had included it in her "Fantasía Mexicana," which she danced on point wearing braids and a *china poblana* (pretty country girl) costume. Sophisticated theatergoers had previously considered the dance comical and lowbrow, but now saw it in a new light. To assure that the jarabe tapatío would become a national symbol of Mexico, the decree stated that it would be taught in the Mexican public schools. The government hoped that with its rousing mariachi music accompaniment it would help define Mexican identity and join the ethnically divided populations.

Meanwhile, the Cristero Wars (1926–1929) caused more upheaval in western Mexico, and many more families fled their villages. Rural residents from Jalisco frequented Tenampa Bar in Plaza Garibaldi in Mexico City to share the pomegranate punch and pozole of their home state. Concho Andrade led the first group hired by the bar to play on the plaza that is now the world center of mariachi. Andrade was also the first mariachi with a regular venue in Mexico City. However, most mariachis, regardless of their hopes for a better life in the city, had a hard time finding work. Seen as little more than vagrants, they faced harassment from the police and were banned from playing in the streets.

In 1926, Dr. Luis Rodríguez, a director of public health from Jalisco, arranged a recording session with Victor Records for Mariachi Coculense Rodríguez (adding his

> In 1924, the *jarabe tapatío,* from the state of Jalisco, became Mexico's national dance.

"Poco a Poquito" by Jesús Helguera. Courtesy of Calendarios Landin.

own name to theirs momentarily); they made some of the first electronic recordings in Mexico. The group's leader was Cirilo Marmolejo (1890–1960). Concho Andrade invited Coculense to play in Plaza Garibaldi with him after Marmolejo and his mariachis became deeply discouraged at their lack of work. The two groups took turns, one playing inside the bar while the other played outside. In the course of his time in Mexico City, Marmolejo's group, Mariachi Coculense de Cirilo Marmolejo, grew from a rural mariachi to an urban mariachi able to navigate the multifaceted opportunities of the city.

1930–1940

The '30s were a time of great changes and commercial opportunities for mariachis. Groups expanded not only in popularity but in size, and the advent of mass transportation and communication created an atmosphere wherein urban mariachis became traveling professional musicians. Folklore scholars became interested in mariachi, and groups began to travel as representatives of Mexico. Two different kinds of mariachi developed during this period. Personified by Andrade and Marmolejo's groups, the first type played a huge repertoire for hire by the song *al talón* (see page 65); the second prepared a limited repertoire geared to recording and stage performances. Andrade's mariachi continued its reign in Plaza Garibaldi, while Mariachi Coculense expanded and traveled extensively. During a trip to Chicago, they made their first recordings in the United States. In 1931, Mariachi Coculense appeared in *Santa* (*Saint*), the first talking movie made in Mexico, beginning a trend that would change the course of mariachi music forever.

The era of Lázaro Cárdenas's presidency (1934–1940) was a period of great growth for urban mariachi. Originally

Mariachi and Jalisco are inextricably linked in the minds of most Mexicans.

a poor boy from Michoacán, Cárdenas was a famous champion and protector of the common people, nationalizing the oil industry and outlawing capital punishment. After traveling to Mexico City to play for Cárdenas's inauguration in 1934, Mariachi Vargas decided to emigrate permanently to the city, marking the beginning of the modern era of the most influential and long-lived mariachi in history.

During this time, the legend of Jalisco as the birthplace of mariachi was established. First, the best-known mariachis in Mexico City were from Jalisco. Second, Jalisco was the largest and most powerful political unit in the west of Mexico, and as such, the home to powerful politicians. They hired mariachis to add regional color at parties and national celebrations in the capital, promoting the idea of mariachi as representative of Mexico in general. Consequently, mariachi and Jalisco were inextricably linked in the minds of most Mexicans and "Mariachi de Cocula" became the brand name for all mariachi music. In truth, the urban music and instrumentation that resulted from the interweaving of subregional styles were more hybrids than attributable to any one area.

The educated elite had been taking their cues from Europe and the United States, but the new trend in nationalism suddenly made all things Mexican attractive. Regional and provincial costumes, dances, and music came into vogue. Combined with the entertainment industry's development of ranchera movies and recordings, mariachi musicians willingly assumed the mantle of the "musical symbol of Mexico."

By the mid-1930s, radio signals broadcast mariachi music across the country. Launched by Emilio Azcárraga in

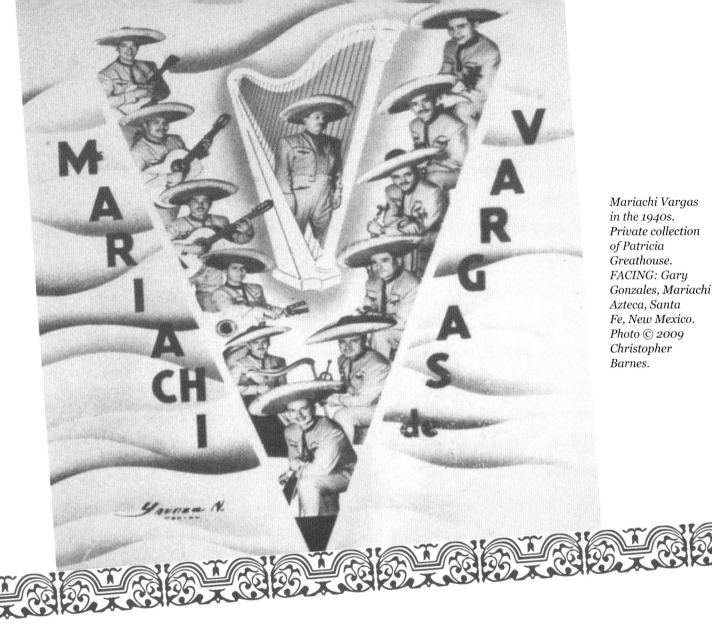

Mariachi Vargas in the 1940s. Private collection of Patricia Greathouse. FACING: Gary Gonzales, Mariachi Azteca, Santa Fe, New Mexico. Photo © 2009 Christopher Barnes.

September 1930, radio station XEW, La Voz de la América Latina desde México (The Voice of Latin America from Mexico), spread the sound of mariachi music not only to remote parts of Mexico, but to Central America and parts of the United States as well.

It featured compelling radio dramas that kept listeners' loyal to the station, and 40 percent of the programming time was dedicated to vernacular music. With radios all over Mexico tuned to the station, the sound of mariachi music became the sound of Mexico.

Radio made Mexico City's singers and mariachi groups famous, as did the movies. In 1934, Tito Guízar starred in Warner Brother's *Allá en el Rancho Grande* (*Out at the Big Ranch*), a rollicking film about country life that started the singing charro genre. The *comedia ranchera* (western comedy) was the Mexican equivalent to the singing cowboy movies in the United States starring artists like Roy Rogers and Gene Autry. In fact, Guízar went on to portray Rogers' sidekick in the Hollywood movie *The Gay Ranchero* in 1948, singing the classic *"Solamente Una Vez (You Belong to My Heart)."*

Mariachi was becoming so popular that—in certain instances—trained musicians began joining groups and specializing in learning a rural sound. The entertainment industry also began to exert a strong influence on the population's musical taste and self-identity. Along with recording studios, they dictated a conformity that produced a recognizable form, the *canción ranchera* (country-style song). Songs became a standard two and a half to three minutes, much shorter than traditional versions because of the limitations of recording technology. Educated musicians arranged versions of traditional provincial pieces and composed songs in the style of folk music. The best artists in the country sang live from Mexico City and the best mariachis, instead of being complete within themselves, became back-up musicians to singing stars.

Hasta Que Perdió Jalisco, *starring Jorge Negrete and Gloria Marin (1945). Private collection of Patricia Greathouse.*

Cirilo Marmolejo's nephew, José Marmolejo (1908–1958), played with his uncle's Mariachi Coculense for many years. He then broke away and started his own group, Mariachi Tapatío, which became wildly popular. As well as adding huapango to the mariachi repertoire, Mariachi Tapatío was innovative in several ways. The group had members who could read music and had studied music theory. Jesús Salazar, their virtuosic trumpet player, has become known as the father of mariachi trumpet.

Mariachi Tapatío began appearing in movies in 1937. Their first picture, *Jalisco Nunca Pierde (Jalisco Never Loses)*, helped establish mariachi as a national form.

1940–1950

Prohibitions against mariachis playing in the streets ended in 1940 by order of President Cárdenas at the end of his term as president. Some historians questions why he waited so long.

The *charro cantor* (singing cowboy) genre dominated the recording and movie industry during the years before and after World War II and gave mariachis an identifiable persona and a musical niche. The relatively new urban population was still nostalgic for country life, and the comedia ranchera movies focused the national consciousness on a shared idyllic past, projected on the screen and largely fictional. Composers and arrangers drew on the wealth of traditional folk tunes and idioms for inspiration, crafting canciones rancheras that sounded like überversions of their country cousins. Much like designer versions of peasant dresses, the fabric was finer and the grubby edges disappeared as educated composers transformed country tunes to city tastes. The entertainment industry had inadvertently accomplished the government's long-held goal of uniting the Mexican people in a common identity.

Comedia ranchera movies played a huge part in the commercial success and universal popularity of mariachi

Luis Aguilar as singing cowboy in Charro a la Fuerza *(1948). Private collection of Patricia Greathouse.*

music. Movies were the most easily affordable entertainment in a poor country, and the Mexican film industry went into full swing in the '40s, producing an astounding number of high-quality, music-filled comedias rancheras that could compete with cinema produced anywhere in the world. Stars like Jorge Negrete and Pedro Infante (page 42–45) became cinema idols, and their songs were backed by mariachis. Mariachi Vargas alone appeared in more than 200 films.

In 1944, Rubén Fuentes (page 58) joined Mariachi Vargas. He brought an even higher sophistication and refinement to mariachi music while keeping the country flavor.

With the onset of the U.S. involvement in World War II, Hollywood went to war. It turned its attention away from making films for entertainment and began making propaganda and training films for the armed forces. The sudden dearth of Hollywood films created a vacuum in Latin America that Mexico filled, and the golden era of Mexican cinema flourished.

1950–1960

In 1951, Miguel Martínez (page 54) left Mariachi Vargas because of conflicts with Silvestre Vargas and frustrated because the trumpet was still struggling for acceptance in mariachi music. He joined Mariachi Mexico de Pepe Villa, a new mariachi made up of former members of Mariachi Pulido, an established group. Villa was interested in developing a two-trumpet sound, and Martínez worked with Jesús Córdoba on two-trumpet harmony, practicing for hours a day to refine the style that now defines modern mariachi trumpet. After a year, Martínez returned to Vargas where he continued as the only trumpet for years.

By the middle of the twentieth century, the instrumentation of modern mariachi was fully developed. The history of mariachi since that time is contained in the stories of individuals, groups, the education movement in the United States, and the advent of women into mixed group mariachis.

Mariachi Mexico de Pepe Villa. Private collection of Patricia Greathouse.

MARIACHI MEXICO DE PEPE VILLA

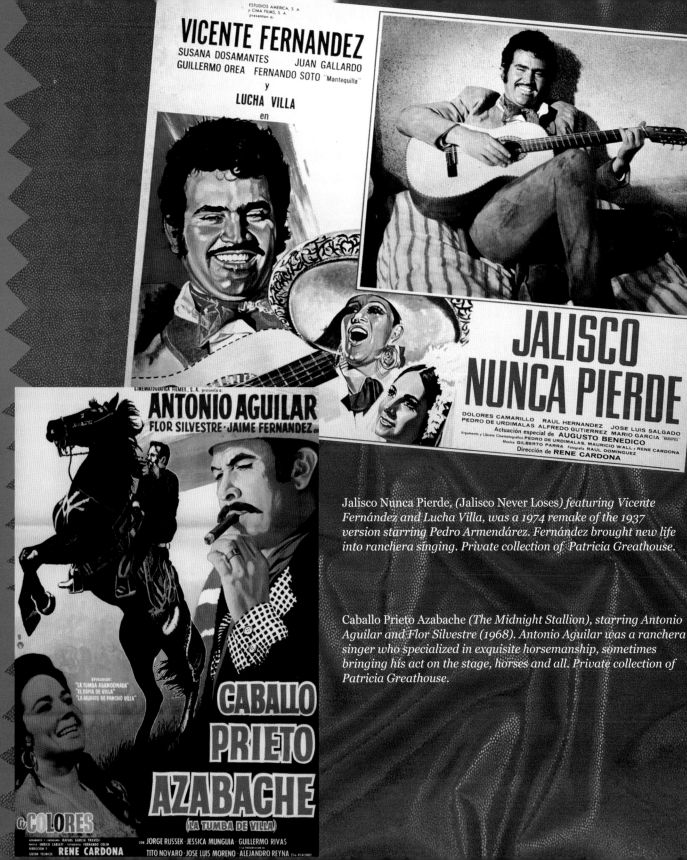

ESTUDIOS AMÉRICA, S. A.
y CIMA FILMS, S. A.
presentan a

VICENTE FERNANDEZ

SUSANA DOSAMANTES   JUAN GALLARDO
GUILLERMO OREA   FERNANDO SOTO "Mantequilla"

y

LUCHA VILLA

en

JALISCO NUNCA PIERDE

DOLORES CAMARILLO   RAUL HERNANDEZ   JOSE LUIS SALGADO
PEDRO DE URDIMALAS   ALFREDO GUTIERREZ   MARIO GARCIA "HARAPOS"
Actuación especial de AUGUSTO BENEDICO
Argumento y Libreto Cinematográfico PEDRO DE URDIMALAS, MAURICIO WALL, y RENE CARDONA
Música GILBERTO PARRA   Fotografía RAUL DOMINGUEZ
Dirección de RENE CARDONA

CINEMATOGRAFICA FILMEX, S. A. presenta a:

ANTONIO AGUILAR

FLOR SILVESTRE · JAIME FERNANDEZ en

EPISODIOS:
"LA TUMBA ABANDONADA"
"EL ESPIA DE VILLA"
"LA MUERTE DE PANCHO VILLA"

CABALLO PRIETO AZABACHE
(LA TUMBA DE VILLA)

oCOLORES

ARGUMENTO Y ORIGINAL RAFAEL GARCIA TRAVESI
MUSICA ENRICO CABIATI   FOTOGRAFIA FERNANDO COLIN
DIRECCION Y
GUION TECNICO
RENE CARDONA

CON JORGE RUSSEK · JESSICA MUNGUIA · GUILLERMO RIVAS
TITO NOVARO · JOSE LUIS MORENO · ALEJANDRO REYNA (1a PLACIBO)

Jalisco Nunca Pierde, (Jalisco Never Loses) featuring Vicente Fernández and Lucha Villa, was a 1974 remake of the 1937 version starring Pedro Armendárez. Fernández brought new life into ranchera singing. Private collection of Patricia Greathouse.

Caballo Prieto Azabache (The Midnight Stallion), starring Antonio Aguilar and Flor Silvestre (1968). Antonio Aguilar was a ranchera singer who specialized in exquisite horsemanship, sometimes bringing his act on the stage, horses and all. Private collection of Patricia Greathouse.

INSTRUMENTS AND SONG FORMS

Traditional rural mariachi music groups used a variety of instruments and musicians. Small folk ensembles from Jalisco were made up of a combination of violin, harp, vihuela, or guitarrón. In parts of western Mexico, the harp and/or guitarrón played the bass part.

Between the first years of the twentieth century and the middle of the century, the instrumentation of modern groups became largely standardized in the *armonía* (rhythm), brass, and violin sections. The armonía section is driven by the guitarrón, guitar, and a percussive vihuela. The violins and trumpets play the melody. In many show and traditional mariachis, the *arpa jalisciense* (harp) doubles the guitarrón bass part and plays virtuosic solo riffs, too.

In rare instances, mariachi groups customize their ensemble. At least one contemporary mariachi, Mariachi Sol de América, adds the requinto (member of the guitar family used in trios) and the guitarra de golpe to their ensemble. Mariachi Divas adds percussion instruments from different Latino cultures; Mariachi Los Halcones from Cuba uses congas, güiros, and other rhythm instruments.

LAS CUERDAS
THE STRINGS

The stringed-instrument family originated with ancient Egyptian lutes and spread throughout Asia, Africa, the Indian subcontinent, and Europe. Attaining regional diversity, the string family developed countless permutations and variety. All early stringed instruments were plucked like a lyre; the bow was a later innovation that has been attributed to Mongol horsemen, who had easy access to the long horsehair required for bows.

Many stringed instruments rely on a hollow box, usually made of wood, for resonance and on strings to produce the sound vibration. Some, like guitars, use frets (raised bars on the fingerboard that delineate the half steps); others, like the violin family, are unfretted, allowing subtle changes in pitch. All are tuned with pegs or metal machine tuners. When mariachis play concerts, stringed instruments use external microphones. Aficionados find mariachi music most appealing when it is played acoustically, and a good sound engineer will try to reproduce the natural timbre of the instruments.

THE VIOLIN

The violin family emerged in the late fifteenth century in Europe, but reached its high point with Amati and Stradivarius, the master luthiers of Cremona, Italy. Their models are still studied extensively and copied by contemporary violin makers all over the world.

The violin has four strings, all tuned in perfect fifths. For modern mariachi playing, most violinists use a wrapped synthetic core string. The instrument top is typically spruce; the back, maple; and the fingerboard, ebony. The sound and tone quality of a violin depend largely on the quality of the wood, the skill of the maker, and the age of the violin. With the advent of the Suzuki violin program, factories began producing violins from full size down to one-thirty-second size—small enough for a three-year-old to play. Today, huge factories in Japan and China turn out economically priced instruments that comprise most of the student violins used in mariachi programs in the United States.

For ideal balance, a mariachi group requires at least three violins to each trumpet. The violins typically play in two- or three-part harmony, either in tandem with or alternating with the trumpets.

Joe Baca, Los Arrieros. Photo © 2009 Christopher Barnes.

ABOVE: Guitarras Chema at the Ciudadela market in Mexico City. Photo © 2009 Madeleine de Sinety. MIDDLE: A vihuelist of Mariachi Las Águilas, El Parián, Tlaquepaque, Mexico. Photo © 2009 Patricia Greathouse. BELOW: Guitarrón, El Numero 1, Mexico City. Photo © 2009 Madeleine de Sinety.

LA ARMONÍA
THE RHYTHM SECTION

THE GUITAR

The classical guitar is one of three rhythm instruments in the armonía section. It replaced the traditional guitarra de golpe. It has six strings and is played with a pick.

Antonio Torres Jurado refined dimensions of the modern guitar in the 1850s in Seville, Spain. In Mexico, the small mountain town of Paracho is the center of guitar making, and their guitars are found in almost every market. Usually made of spruce, cedar, mahogany, or *palo escrito* (Mexican rosewood), only the best materials are used in the finest Mexican-made guitars, and performers come from all over the world to buy from the masters of Paracho. As with violins, the guitar varies widely in quality depending on workmanship and materials.

THE VIHUELA

The vihuela has five nylon strings and a convex back; it also plays rhythm in the mariachi armonía section. Players often grow their fingernails long on the right hand, use fingertip picks, or glue acrylic nails to their fingertips to help them produce the particularly strident and percussive sound for which the vihuela is known.

Although it shares the same name as the Spanish guitar ancestor (a vihuela brought to the Americas by Cortéz), the Mexican vihuela comes from the Ameca-Cocula area of central Jalisco.

THE GUITARRÓN

The guitarrón, also probably from the Ameca-Cocula area and intrinsic to mariachi music, is similar to an oversized vihuela. Made of *tacote* (a light Mexican native wood similar to balsa) and other light woods, the six-string, unfretted guitarrón is held by a strap that goes over the player's shoulders and around the back. A guitarronero plucks two notes at a time in octaves from the heavy-gauge strings. As the portable acoustic bass of the armonía section, it's the group's center and heartbeat.

THE TRUMPET

The trumpet is the highest-pitched member of the brass family and the only member of the mariachi ensemble that is not a stringed instrument. Its history dates back to 1500 BC; crude trumpets have been found in the tombs of ancient pharaohs. Originally, the harsh sound of primitive trumpets was used mainly for signaling and religious purposes, not for music.

Musicians use a cupped mouthpiece to blow air through their closed lips, producing a buzz that creates standing-wave vibrations inside the trumpet. The pitch can be modified by changing the embouchure (lip opening and tension) or by depressing the three valves. Mariachi trumpeters are famous for their well-developed embouchures.

The Mexican military used trumpets, and many battalions had their own bands. The trumpet made incursions into mariachi groups before the 1940s and became part of the modern mariachi ensemble after much public resistance. Today, a mariachi group is considered incomplete without at least one trumpet.

THE HARP

An essential part of many traditional mariachi ensembles, the mariachi harp, also known as the Jalisco harp, is now found mainly in small-town mariachis and show groups. The guitarrón replaced the harp early on because it is more portable and plays in different keys more easily than the harp.

The mariachi harp's charming, distinctive, and resonant sound plays bass lines and chords as well as sparkling instrumental solos. Harps vary physically depending on the desires of the maker and the player, but they are all relatively strong and light with thirty-six strings. Often made of tacote and cedar, they were traditionally strung with gut, but today's harps use nylon strings. Stuck in diatonic tuning, the harpist can neither play chromatically nor change the key readily and must use his or her thumb to shorten the string to change pitch a semi-tone on the bass strings. The relative inflexibility of the mariachi harp contributed to the guitarrón's popularity. When mariachis became more urban, driving to performances or working *al talón* in cantinas, it became clear that the size of a harp was a hindrance.

BASIC SONG FORMS IN MARIACHI

The first mariachi music came from western Mexico, but modern mariachis have borrowed regional music from other parts of Mexico, Latin America, the Caribbean, the United States, and Europe. Beginning from the epicenter of western Mexico and expanding outward, the following song forms are the types of pieces performed by modern mariachis.

THE SON

The *son* is Mexico's most common folk music and the son jalisciense is the classic music of the mariachis. Although the definition is hard to pin down, it is probably safe to say that its roots are Andalusian gypsy combined with Mexican indigenous elements with an African beat. Sones commonly alternate between $\frac{6}{8}$ and $\frac{3}{4}$ rhythms.

The *zapateado* (stamped foot step) is the dance that celebrates the son. Exciting syncopated rhythms, full, fast bow strokes on the violins, and punctuated trumpet parts define the *son jalisciense*. "La Negra," called

ABOVE: Mariachi Sol de Mexico trumpeter from El Paso, Texas. Mariachi Spectacular Student Showcase, Albuquerque, New Mexico. Photo © 2009 Christopher Barnes. BELOW: Jalisco harp, Mariachi Nuevo Tecalitlán of Guadalajara, 2007. Photo © 2009 Patricia Greathouse.

the mariachi national anthem, is perhaps the most well known of the sones.

THE JARABE

By government decree, the jarabe has been the national dance of Mexico since 1924. The best known is the "Jarabe Tapatío," known in the United States as the "Mexican Hat Dance."

Descended from the fifteenth-century Spanish *jarabe gatuno*, it was modified by indigenous influences and has been danced in the west of Mexico since the eighteenth century. The jarabe is a medley of dance pieces that depicts courtship, and as such, was once frowned upon by the Catholic church for its licentiousness!

THE RANCHERA

A sentimental Mexican country-style song, the canción ranchera is also known more simply as ranchera. Everyone knows *"Cielito Lindo* (Beautiful Heaven)," with its "ay, yay, yay, yay, canta y no llores," as well as "Allá en el Rancho Grande." Both are favorite requests of every tourist who has ever crossed the border. The ranchera genre holds some of the most heartbreaking songs of lost love and longing—*"Mi Ranchito* (My Little Shanty)"—as well as some of the most upbeat celebratory songs of pride—*"El Herradero* (The Round-up)." Canción ranchera composition soared during the golden age of Mexican cinema in the 1940s, and then José Alfredo Jiménez gave the canción ranchera new life during the early 1950s and Vicente Fernandez spurred its popularity again a decade later.

Ranchera is perhaps the most widely performed genre in the mariachi repertoire. Many pop singers, conjunto, banda, rock, and jazz bands record ranchera music, adapting them to their own particular region and style.

THE CORRIDO

Ranchera's older cousin is the *corrido*. Descended from an old Spanish form, the corrido was a way of passing along news or legends in a narrative, epic form. In the times before newspapers were widely distributed, they gave lively, memorable accounts of interesting people and events. In revolutionary Mexico, corridos told stories of heroes, bandits, horses, and towns—in short, anything newsworthy. Verses might be added along the way, and a moralizing ending often advised others to avoid the actions described in the song in order to escape a similar fate. A favorite corrido, *"El Caballo Blanco* (The White Horse)" by José Alfredo Jiménez, tells the story of his journey in a big white luxury car—Cadillac or Lincoln, depending on the source—through the towns in the northwest of Mexico; the car and driver are, of course, a metaphor for a horse and rider.

THE CHOTIS

The *chotis* descended from the Bohemian *schottische*. (In Bohemia it is thought of as a Scottish dance.) A couples' dance that spread all over Europe in many variations during the nineteenth century, it is well represented in Mexico by *"Trompetas del Diablo* (The Devil's Trumpets)."* Interestingly, in Spain the most popular chotis is "Madrid, Madrid, Madrid" by Mexican bolero composer Agustín Lara.

THE MARCH

Marches are a necessary part of Mexican and Mexican-American social and political events. In New Mexico, marriages are not complete without *"La Marcha de Zacatecas* (The Zacatecas March)," by Genaro Codina Fernández; it begins with a familiar trumpet fanfare that calls all guests to join the parade around the dance floor.

THE BOLERO

Boleros, with their rich harmonies and romantic themes, are the deluxe creamy filling of the mariachi pie. They can

Mariachi Juvenil de Santa Fe plays polka "Jesusita en Chihuahua" for dancers Adrianna Romp and Mariah Garcia. Photo © 2009 Christopher Barnes.

Folkloric dancers dance to a son in Student Showcase of Albuquerque Mariachi Spectacular, New Mexico. Photo © 2009 Christopher Barnes.

melt the hardest heart and bring tears to the coldest eyes. Originating in Spain, the bolero became an Afro-Cuban song and dance form. Boleros worked their way through the Caribbean to Mexico, changing character as they went.

Trios like Los Tres Ases and Trio los Panchos originally made boleros popular in Mexico. Miguel Aceves Mejía scorned the bolero as not Mexican (although he recorded them); Javier Solís became an idol singing them. Agustín Lara wrote the most well-known bolero, "Solamente una Vez (You Belong to My Heart)." However, a woman, Consuelo Velazquez, wrote one of the finest and most-played boleros, "Besame Mucho (Kiss Me Again and Again)," when she was a chaste convent girl.

THE HUAPANGO

Huapango, from San Luis Potosi and Hidalgo, has a complex rhythm (alternating twos and threes in a six-beat or $\frac{12}{8}$ measure), which includes syncopation and offbeats. Huapangos showcase improvisational and virtuosic violin playing, complete with ricochet bowing and triad chords. The team of arranger Rubén Fuentes, singer Miguel Aceves Mejía, and songwriter José Alfredo Jiménez brought huapango to its highest and most dramatic incarnation, highlighting falsetto passages, stirring accompaniment, and moving lyrics. Mejía's interpretation of "El Pastor (The Shepherd)" is one of the great songs of the genre.

THE SON JAROCHO

The *son jarocho* comes from the southern part of Veracruz where it is traditionally highly improvisational; however, mariachi arrangements of son jarochos are standardized. Distinguished by its percussive armonía style and syncopation, it is probably the Mexican son style most influenced by African rhythms. One of the favorite mariachi son jarochos is the virtuosic *"El Cascabel,"* which gives each instrumental section a chance to play a flashy solo.

THE DANZON

The *danzón*, a genre borrowed from a popular Afro-Cuban dance form, is most popular in the Yucatan peninsula, but old clubs still exist catering to aficionados in the big cities. "Juarez" is a popular mariachi danzón number.

THE CUMBIA

Borrowed from Colombia, the *cumbia* is wildly popular dance music in Mexico and parts of the United States. Some mariachi purists detest it and ban it from competitions during conferences, but it is much requested, especially the ubiquitous *"El Mariachi Loco (The Crazy Mariachi)"* written by Roman Palomar.

THE JOROPO

The *joropo* is filled with complex, jazz-inflected chords placed against $\frac{3}{4}$ - $\frac{6}{8}$ shifts and syncopation. The genre pushed mariachi music into a more modern, experimental, sophisticated stage. Joropo requires technical skill, and songs like Fuentes's *"La Bikina"* are regular requests.

THE PASODOBLE

The *pasodoble,* an old mariachi style inherited from Spain, recreates the drama of the bullfight. It's based on music played when the torero enters the ring and on the passes just before the kill. Trumpets play brilliant fanfares, and violin parts are sweeping and lyrical, depicting the pageantry of a day of *sangre y sol* (blood and sun). "*El Dos Negro* (The Black Two)" is a well-known pasodoble.

THE WALTZ

El Valse, the waltz, originated in Vienna about 1780, but quickly spread through the rest of Europe, and came to Mexico during the French intervention. Although now considered a dance for refined retirees, waltzes were at one time condemned by the church as decadent because of the belly-to-belly stance of the partners. The 3-beat measure with the emphasis on the first beat initiates the long-quick-quick dance step.

"Viva Mi Desgracia (Long Live My Misfortune)" by Francisco Cárdenas is a lovely waltz with varying rhythms in the manner of Johann Strauss, the Viennese waltz king.

THE POLKA

Polcas (polkas), are instrumental dance pieces from Bohemia and probably arrived in Mexico during the French Intervention. Common in the north of Mexico and the southwestern United States, their fast $\frac{2}{4}$ rhythms inspire dancers and put smiles on their faces. The most familiar polka in mariachi repertoire is "Jesusita en Chihuahua," a catchy piece composed of several distinct parts that give the violins and trumpets each a chance to solo.

THE POTPOURRI

The potpourri is a popular way of presenting a variety of pieces, either of a single composer or theme. It's a way of showing off talent and virtuosity. When mariachis compete against each other in timed events and at mariachi conferences, potpourris are a good way to give a sampling of songs. Mariachi Vargas's "Viva Veracruz I, II, and III" are excellent examples of the potpourri genre.

THE MARIACHI SINFÓNICO

One of the most exciting new challenges for top show mariachis began in the late eighties when groups like Marichi

Folkloric dancers perform to son "El Gavilancillo," at the Las Cruces International Mariachi Conference. Photo © 2009 Christopher Barnes.

Vargas de Tecalitlán, Mariachi Cobre, and Mariachi Sol de Mexico began playing pops concerts with symphony orchestras. Mariachis had long included classical pieces in their repertoires, and *mariachi sinfónico* not only gave classical music audiences exposure to Mexican music and to professional mariachi groups, it also gave mariachis a chance to show their versatility and musicianship. Once derided and disrespected by classical musicians, top-tier mariachis now find their place at home in symphony halls all over the world.

SCREEN STARS AND EARLY MARIACHIS

The cinema industry and especially comedia ranchera was immensely important for the formation and advancement of modern mariachi. Films about the revolution of 1910 were some of the first important themes of the Mexican cinema, while movies about families, swashbucklers, westerns, and comedies were made for pure entertainment.

Comedia ranchera began with a release in 1935 of *Allá en el Rancho Grande*. The genre responded to a national longing for the country's rural past. The Mexican Revolution, the Cristero Wars, the subsequent economic upheaval due to destruction of villages during the wars, and land reform had been the impetus for a huge population migration to the cities.

Comedia ranchera romanticized notions of a bucolic rural past. It helped define Mexico's national identity visually, emotionally, and musically. Initially conceived as a parody, comedia ranchera was inspired in part by *zarzuela* (Spanish light opera), a traveling entertainment well known throughout the country. The genre was extremely popular, and countless permutations on like themes were produced, all full of folk music, rural costumes, simple humor, beautiful horses, and cross-country chases. The men were pistol-wielding machos, strugglers against injustice, or fatally attractive bad boys. The women were either scheming heartbreakers or *flores silvestres* (wildflowers)—simple, brave, and full of modest virtue. Some stood by their men and kept the home fires burning; others ruined the men who adored them. The subject matter was perfectly expressed through mariachi music.

The names of the idols of the Mexican cinema still evoke love, reverence, and awe. Larger than life, they propelled the Mexican entertainment industry to its zenith during the '30s, '40s, and '50s. They weren't mariachis, but the traje de charro–wearing stars institutionalized the uniform and turned the canción ranchera into the national music of Mexico.

The dreamy faces, rich voices, and charismatic personalities of Jorge Negrete, Pedro Infante, Miguel Aceves Mejía, and Javier Solís made them huge stars, and their recordings and movies provided employment and public exposure for the best mariachis.

Eventually, mariachis began fronting their own groups, becoming huge attractions and recording artists in their own right. The well-loved songs from the golden age of the Mexican cinema became a large part of their repertoire. In fact, many of the songs were written by mariachis. The classic recordings are now an integral part of the Mexican patrimony, the songs most requested at mariachi performances.

JORGE NEGRETE

BORN NOVEMBER 30, 1911, GUANAJUATO, GUANAJUATO, MEXICO
DIED DECEMBER 5, 1953, LOS ANGELES, CALIFORNIA, UNITED STATES

The Mexican movie industry was just beginning when Jorge Negrete began his acting career in the mid-1930s. He played larger-than-life heroes and villains in cornball formulaic comedia ranchera vehicles, which gave him a platform for his bel canto–style singing voice.

Negrete was notoriously proud of his *hacendado* (wealthy land-owning) roots. His father was an army officer who dragged his family from town to town while his platoon fought revolutionaries. While peasants were fighting for land reform and to right the injustices of the *patrón* system, young Negrete enrolled in the military academy, took singing lessons, and dreamt of being an opera star. He experienced one frightening, grim battle as a soldier in the government army and decided he far preferred singing to fighting.

With a reputation for being arrogant and difficult, Negrete often made bad professional decisions based on pride. Initially, he considered dressing in costume to be beneath his dignity, but ironically, he made his name as El Charro Cantor, the singing horseman. As Mexico's first internationally famous idol, Negrete became rich and beloved in the Spanish-speaking world and eventually married the great Mexican film star María Félix.

As Mexico's first idol, everything about Negrete was fascinating to the public. His personal life, his overseas successes, and his women provided fodder for the gossip mills. His long romance with Gloria Marin, for whom he left his first wife, Elisa Christy, assured Marin's stardom. Although Negrete and Marin never married, they were together for over ten years; during that period, he refused roles unless she was cast as his leading lady. Negrete suffered almost constantly from hepatitis, which he had contracted in New York City on his first attempt to make a career in the United States. He stoically ignored his health and worked on, sometimes collapsing on the set. In dire need of money because of troubles associated with his marriage to María Félix, he traveled to Los Angeles. Even though he was weak and ill, he had hopes of making it in

Publicity portrait of Jorge Negrete. Private collection of Patricia Greathouse.

Hollywood. Shortly after arriving in the United States, he collapsed. He died a few days later of a liver hemorrhage. The Mexican government sent a plane to fly Negrete's body back home, and hundreds of thousands of people lined the streets to view his final slow procession through the streets of Mexico City.

The words from his famous recording "*México Lindo y Querido* (Beautiful and Beloved Mexico)" are haunting:

México lindo y querido,
Si muero lejos de ti,
Que digan que estoy
   dormido,
Y que me traigan aquí.

Beautiful and beloved Mexico,
If I die far from you,
Have them say that I'm only
   dreaming,
And have them bring me here.

PEDRO INFANTE

BORN NOVEMBER 18, 1917, MAZATLÁN, SINALOA
DIED APRIL 15, 1957, NEAR MÉRIDA, YUCATÁN, MEXICO

Pedro Infante was self-effacing and poor—the epitome of country-boy charm and mexicanismo. He was in many ways Negrete's opposite. Known as *El Muchacho Alegre* (The Happy Boy), Infante used a combination of will, hard work, and personal charisma to attain his success. Although he lacked Negrete's fine singing voice and was a poor actor when he first started out, he soon surpassed the original singing horseman in popularity.

Directors loved to play off the Infante-Negrete rivalry.

In the movie *Dos Tipos de Cuidado (Two Dangerous Characters)*, Negrete plays Jorge Bueno against Infante's Pedro Malo. Both are typecast—contrasting social backgrounds and personality traits duel it out, with love and honor hanging in the balance.

Infante loved motorcycles, model railroads, and airplanes. As an honorary member of the Mexico City motorcycle brigade, he led Jorge Negrete's funeral cortège through the streets of Mexico City. Little did he know that

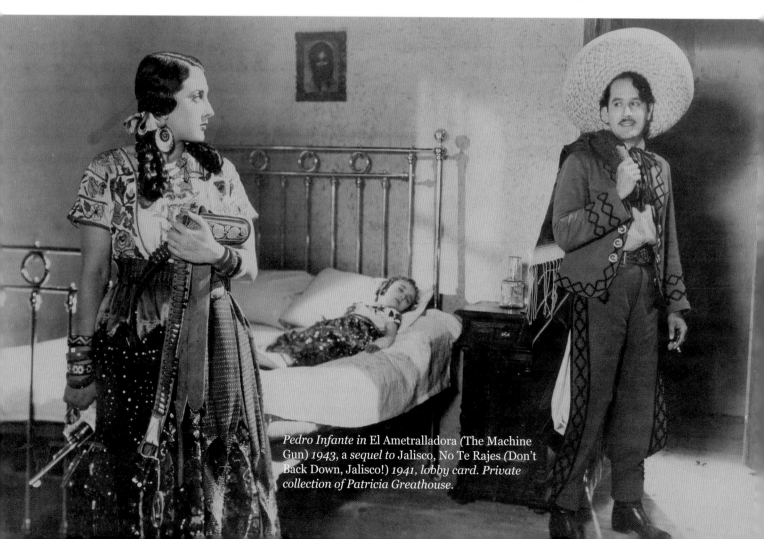

Pedro Infante in El Ametralladora (The Machine Gun) *1943, a sequel to* Jalisco, No Te Rajes (Don't Back Down, Jalisco!) *1941, lobby card. Private collection of Patricia Greathouse.*

his obsession with airplanes would lead to an equally sad procession less than four years later.

Crowds mauled Infante wherever he went. Teeming crowds tore the shirt off his back—everyone wanted to touch him. Although he was exhausted by the attention and suffered from diabetes, he never complained—he felt that he owed the public his success and was unfailingly patient and generous. Infante loved women and children, too, and the precise number of his offspring is unknown, for when very young women were concerned, Infante couldn't resist.

Infante's characterization of the singing cowboy took off where Negrete's left off; his characters became less stereotypical and more developed than the caricatures played by Negrete. He was good at comedy, too; he was a natural clown with winning charm. His recordings and movies made him rich, and he became known as "The Idol of Guamúchil," his birthplace.

Infante had a habit of flying when he was under emotional strain or hurried, and he survived several crashes. His third plane wreck was his last. His plane went into a nosedive outside Mérida, Mexico; he had been on his way to Mexico City to persuade his wife to give him a divorce so that he could remarry. As with Negrete's funeral procession, half a million people lined the streets of Mexico City to say goodbye, and the mariachis played "Las Golondrinas (The Swallows)" at his grave, as he had wished.

MIGUEL ACEVES MEJÍA

Born November 15, 1915, Ciudad Juárez, Chihuahua, Mexico
Died November 6, 2006, Mexico City, Mexico

Known as the king of the falsetto, Miguel Aceves Mejía made some of the most moving and dramatic recordings in the history of Mexican music. He began his professional life as an actor in a traveling theater company, and later recorded music with the trio Los Porteños. In 1945, Mejía decided to dedicate himself to singing. His recordings of huapangos like "El Pastor (The Shepherd)" and "La Malagueña (The Woman from Málaga)" are the high-water mark of the genre. The orchestration of the former piece begins with a lilting flute solo reminiscent of a country pan pipe; the latter, with its fiery introduction, resonates with the gypsy passion of the south of Spain. As one of the men who claimed to have discovered José Alfredo Jiménez, Mejía showed great pride in recognizing the greatness of the humble man who was a waiter when they met. Although later he would say there was no place

Miguel Aceves Mejía. Courtesy of RCA.

in modern mariachi for people who didn't read music, that was exactly the state José Alfredo was in his entire life, and Mejía profited greatly from their association.

Mejía toured extensively throughout Latin America with Mariachi Vargas, drawing large crowds wherever they appeared. He eventually became a regular breakfast guest of President Juan Perón during his tours in Argentina, although when invited to bring along the rest of his entourage—Mariachi Vargas—he declined.

Even though Mejía never attained the level of idolatry that Negrete and Infante enjoyed, he recorded over a thousand songs and acted in over sixty films. At the end of his long and productive life, his body lay in the Palacio de las Bellas Artes (the Palace of Fine Arts) in Mexico City, an honor reserved for the finest artists.

Poster for Viva Chihuahua *(1961) with Miguel Aceves Mejía and Tin Tan. Private collection of Patricia Greathouse.*

Painting of Javier Solís (right) and Pedro Infante (left) in Salon Tenampa, Plaza Garibaldi, Mexico City. Photo © 2009 Jasper Schriber.

JAVIER SOLÍS

BORN SEPTEMBER 1, 1931, MEXICO CITY, MEXICO
DIED APRIL 19, 1966, MEXICO CITY, MEXICO

Javier Solís became the leading interpreter of the bolero ranchera in the late 1950s. His smooth style and beautiful voice were perfect for transmitting all the joys and fears of love. Although he had roles as a singing cowboy on occasion, he was more successful as a singer than a movie star; his style was more urban than the other singing cowboys, and his audience more international.

Born Gabriel Siria Levario, Solís grew up in Tacubaya, a tough part of Mexico City. Abandoned by his father, he worked hard from an early age to help his mother support the family. He was athletic—playing soccer and other sports—and some say he trained as a boxer just to survive on the neighborhood streets.

Solís began his singing career while working as a butcher, entering contests where the prize was a pair of shoes. He finally won so many times that he was disqualified from competing and was paid to sing instead. The boss heard him singing on the job, and encouraged him to quit the butcher shop, paying for lessons with singing teacher Noé Quintero, the coach of many other top singers.

Still working under his given name, Gabriel Siria, Solís formed a trio with friends, and then later worked a bit as a

Filmadora Chapultepec, S.A. presenta a:
Luis AGUILAR Javier SOLIS

LUCHA VILLA · MARTHA ELENA CERVANTES en
AGARRANDO PAREJO

Argumento Adap. JAIME SALVADOR Música: MANUEL ESPERON Dirección: JAIME SALVADOR

Agarrando Parejo (Grabbing a Partner, *1964) with*
Javier Solís and Luis Aguilar, lobby card. Private collection of Patricia Greathouse.

mariachi in Puebla, Mexico. Returning to Mexico City, he worked on Plaza Garibaldi. The members of Los Panchos, a famous trio, eventually discovered him while he was performing at the Azteca Bar.

A contract with CBS Mexico followed, and Solís recorded his first album in 1950. In 1952 he had a big hit with "*Llororas* (You'll Cry)." Felipe Valdez Leal, his producer, encouraged him to change his name, and Gabriel Siria Levario became Javier Solís.

In 1957, the premature death of Pedro Infante left a void that Solís was ready to fill. Although famous for his bolero rancheras, Solís also recorded rancheras, waltzes, and tangos.

Solís, like his predecessors Negrete and Infante, starred and sang in comedia ranchera. *Juan Pistolas (Pistol John,* 1965) was his last movie; he died from complications of a gall bladder operation at the age of 34. Solís's recordings are classics and still sell well around the world.

Infante, Negrete, and Solís all died premature deaths. Like James Dean and Elvis in the United States, rumors and mystery surrounds them, and devoted fans still cling to their memories. There are rumors that Infante faked his death and is living, hidden somewhere in peaceful retreat. Mejía lived to the great age of 91 and many still considered him to be the finest canción ranchera singer who ever lived.

JOSÉ ALFREDO JIMÉNEZ

"EL REY PARA LA ETERNIDAD (THE KING FOR ETERNITY)"

BORN JANUARY 9, 1926, DOLORES HIDALGO, GUANAJUATO, MEXICO
DIED NOVEMBER 23, 1973, MEXICO CITY, MEXICO

Perhaps the most enigmatic of the important influences on modern mariachi, José Alfredo Jiménez was known and loved by colleagues and the public alike; everyone affectionately called him José Alfredo as if they knew him personally. He identified with the common man, but his background seems to have been middle class—his father owned a pharmacy, and his mother came from a well-educated and scholarly family. He sincerely felt compassion for the human condition, and many of his songs speak of the life of the lowly, the heartbroken, and the devastatingly drunk. He also was a master of the idealistic, romantic love song.

The greatest songwriter of the canción ranchera in the history of Mexican music, José Alfredo fueled his genius with *parranda* (merrymaking), women, camaraderie, and vino. Unlike the handsome silken-voiced idols who interpreted his songs, José Alfredo was homely. His voice was rough but expressive and filled with emotion. He turned canción ranchera on its ear by telling the raw emotional truth of life and love without dressing it up in metaphor, and many criticized him for it.

Dolores Hidalgo was the seat of Mexican independence, and it spurred young José Alfredo's imagination. His first song, *"El Jinete* (The Horseman)," written when he was still a child, is rife with drama and dark emotion, telling the haunting story of a horseman who has lost his love and is riding, searching only for his death.

When José Alfredo was eleven years old, his father died, changing the fortunes of the family forever. His mother moved the family from their beloved Dolores Hidalgo to Mexico City, where she opened a little shop. She was not a good businesswoman, however, and José Alfredo delivered papers, waited tables, and sang in a trio to help make ends meet. Never trained as a musician, he did manage to learn to sing well enough to earn money in neighborhood cantinas.

There are several stories of how José Alfredo was discovered, and they all probably contributed to forwarding his career. It's certainly true in his case that "Success has a thousand mothers, while failure is an orphan."

José Alfredo's life provided the raw ingredients for his songs. While still a teenager, his girlfriend wronged him, and it inspired the song "Ella." Thus began the theme of deception and betrayal that appears with such frequency in his work. It's clear from his early lyrics that José Alfredo was already familiar with the practice of drowning his sorrows, a habit that foreshadowed his demise.

When his brother died in Guanajuato, José Alfredo wrote the song *"Camino de Guanajuato* (The Road to Guanajuato)" the day of the funeral service. In it are the famous lines, *"No vale nada la vida, La vida no vale nada* (Life is worth nothing)."

José Alfredo's life was not only *rica en canción* (rich in song); it was rich in love in all its aspects. He married Paloma Gálvez, one of his earliest supporters, and was inspired to write *"Guitarras de Medianoche* (Midnight Guitars)" for her. Many women artists were deeply attracted to him and his compositions. Lola Beltrán was an important interpreter of his rancheras; her recordings were huge commercial successes.

Lucha Villa often was José Alfredo's preferred partner onstage and off, and he was inspired to write some of his most idealistic and optimistic love songs based on their clandestine relationship, including "*Si Nos Dejan* (If They Let Us)."

The prospect of becoming one of José Alfredo's muses must have been a strong aphrodisiac, and his poetic soul, kindly nature, and inspiring turn of phrase surely did more to capture the hearts of women than his substantial wealth and success. The love songs he wrote explored the gamut of relationships: idolatry, anger, envy, devotion, and frustration. In "*La Mano de Dios* (The Hand of God)," "only the hand of God can separate us," he sings. The sweet sincerity of this song makes it a favorite request at every wedding.

Porque todos se entregan,	Because everyone
borrachos de amor en el	surrenders,
mundo.	Drunk on love in this world.

José Alfredo published over 400 songs and made countless recordings. His collaboration with Rubén Fuentes, who arranged many of his songs, and Miguel Aceves Mejía, perhaps his best male interpreter, produced

Lucha Reyes in Los Amores de Juan Charrasqueado *(The Loves of Juan Charrasqueado, 1968), lobby card. Private collection of Patricia Greathouse.*

examples of the best classic mariachi music. Mariachi Vargas de Tecalitlán accompanied the stellar recordings.

As with many modern, passionate young men, José Alfredo spent time as a bohemian. He seems to have agreed with the German philosopher Friedrich Nietzsche's existentialist philosophy that tragedy could be seen as an affirmation of life. Many of his songs also seem to express an existentialist overlay on the historical fatalism of the Mexican male, the attitude that everything is broken or going to fail anyway, so why bother, let's have another tequila.

MI TENAMPA

CUAL CARIÑO ES EL QUE DICES
QUE TE DI CON TODA EL ALMA
CUANDO ABRISTE TU CONMIGO
LAS PERSIANAS DEL TENAMPA

TU QUE SABES DE LA VIDA
TU QUE ENTIENDES POR PASIONES
TU CUANDO OYES UN MARIACHI
NI COMPRENDES SUS CANCIONES

PARRANDA Y TENAMPA
MARIACHI Y CANCIONES
ASI ES COMO VIVO YO

YO ME PARO EN LAS CANTINAS
Y A SALUD DE LAS INGRATAS
HAGO QUE SE SIRVA VINO
PA' QUE NAZCAN SERENATAS

Y UNA VEZ YA BIEN SERVIDO
VOY CON RUMBO DEL TENAMPA
Y Y AHI ME AGARRO A MI MARIACHI
Y A CANTAR CON TODO EL ALMA
TU QUE SABES DE LA VIDA
DE LA VIDA ENTRE LAS COPAS
TU PA'SER MI CONSENTIDA
NECESITAS MUCHAS COSAS

José Alfredo Jiménez

Painting of José Alfredo Jiménez and the words to his song "Mi Tenampa" on the wall of Salon Tenampa, Plaza Garibaldi, Mexico City. Photo © 2009 Jasper Schriber.

José Alfredo appeared on *Siempre en Domingo (Always on Sunday)*, a popular television show broadcast from Mexico City) on November 11, 1973, to sing *"Gracias* (Thank You)." "Gracias" was his last song and expressed sincere, heartfelt thanks to his fans.

José Alfredo entered a Mexico City clinic right after his television appearance and was dead by November 28 of cirrhosis and a bleeding ulcer, souvenirs of his long romance with vino. As with Negrete and Infante, the public turned out en masse to bid farewell to one of their own.

José Alfredo wished to be buried in his hometown of Dolores Hidalgo, not in the Grand Pantheon of Illustrious Men in Mexico City. His simple headstone was a mesquite marker and the words *"La vida no vale nada."* Twenty-five years later, fans insisted that he be moved to a grander mausoleum.

In 1993, twenty years after José Alfredo's death, Chavela Vargas won recognition for best record of the year in Germany for an album of José Alfredo's songs, proving that his artistic achievement and their collaboration survived beyond the grave.

LIVING LEGENDS

Miguel Martínez, Mexico City, December, 2006. Photo © 2009 Christopher Barnes. BELOW: Mariachi Tolteca. Private Collection of Patricia Greathouse.

When conferences began in the United States in the late 1970s, a small group of veteran musicians started making trips across the border to teach. Each musician was accomplished and held an important position in the refinement of modern mariachi in Mexico; they all had written the arrangements and played on many recordings. They were gracious, humble, and dignified; at the conferences they found recognition and honor at a time when mariachi music was declining in Mexico.

These *maestros* (master teachers) came from a tradition where only young men became mariachis. They express wonder and gratitude that there are students now of all ages, both genders, and every ethnicity who are passionate about learning to play mariachi music.

MIGUEL MARTÍNEZ

Born 1921, Celaya, Guanajuato, Mexico

Many consider Miguel Martínez the greatest mariachi trumpet stylist in history; few know that he also composed some of the best-known pieces in the mariachi repertoire and appeared in over 120 films. He saw the growth of mariachi through Mariachi Vargas's golden period and has been deeply involved in mariachi education in the United States from the beginning. He is well loved and respected for his kind and generous nature and his supreme musicianship.

As a child, Martínez ran behind the mariachis as they played in his Mexico City neighborhood. He began trumpet when he was thirteen years old, although he also learned to play guitar.

Martínez studied classical technique to become skilled. He loved the music of the big bands, and Tommy Dorsey, Stan Kenton, and Glenn Miller were his idols. He also became a member of the musicians' union, studying hard to pass the music dictation part of the test, a skill that was invaluable for composition.

Around 1936, Martínez began playing with mariachis in Plaza Garibaldi, subbing in Concho Andrade's Tenampa Bar mariachi. About 1940, he joined Mariachi Vargas de Tecalitlán as their trumpeter. Here's his tale of how two trumpets came to be used in mariachi music a decade later:

> When I worked with Silvestre Vargas's Mariachi Vargas, I had to stand around, not playing because the patrons didn't want the trumpet. I was upset, so I went for my professional test to join the musicians' union. I didn't want to return to mariachi.
>
> Pedro Infante had already recorded with two trumpets and what happened? The public didn't like it, so the recording company withdrew it.

> About that time, it turned out that a new radio station started—XEX— as competition for XEW. Pepe Villa decided to use two trumpets, and he offered me the job playing for XEX. He wanted to innovate, and he made me a good offer. I played the first trumpet part and my compañero Jesús Córdoba played second. Villa took a chance using two trumpets, and the people didn't want even one! Listeners didn't like it, and they phoned into the radio station and sent cards, too, saying, "What's going on?" What were we to do? The public was very conservative—they wanted the mariachi as it had always been. It was a landmark for the mariachi trumpet, for Pepe Villa was the first man to have two trumpets playing in two parts in his group.

When he retired from Mariachi Vargas in 1965, Martínez had been part of the landmark recordings of their *epoca de oro* (golden period). He went on to play in many more groups and on many more recordings.

Martínez's first composition was "*La Prieta Ingrata*," recorded by a rough country-style singer named Francisco Charro Avitia, "*El Voz del Corrido* (The Voice of Corrido)." Many more compositions and movies followed.

After Martínez heard a marching band in a parade in Indianapolis, he began using the marches in his compositions. "I love the music of John Philip Sousa. I put in things from him—the master!" "*Café Colon* (Columbus Café)," the theme of a movie by the same name, and "*La Chuparrosa* (The Hummingbird)," also a movie theme, have distinct Sousa-sounding introductions. Martínez says the many marches he wrote were always popular.

I've been lucky because God gave me the opportunity to go out into the world. One year I lived in Paris; I lived in the neighborhood of Montparnasse, Los Invalides, and the Acapulco Club. I met Anthony Quinn and Edith Piaf. They used to come to the club where I was playing. A man in the audience loved "El Son de La Culebra." He asked, "What's it called?" We said, "La Culebra. The Snake!" He said, "Play it again!" He was the visiting conductor of the Paris orchestra. Those people really liked the sones and huapangos!

I also lived a year in Spain. I went to Buenos Aires with Miguel Aceves Mejía and Pedro Infante. They still play the music of Jorge Negrete there. I go each year to the University of New Mexico to teach the sones of Jalisco. I have to tell them how to put in the accents and the flavor. The word "mariachi" used to mean a low kind of person, but Silvestre Vargas changed that perception. His discipline was very vigorous. I went to the White House with Silvestre Vargas when Roosevelt was in office—we were the first mariachis to play there.

Miguel Martínez retired from Mariachi Vargas in 1965 but hasn't stopped performing. He continues to practice his trumpet, play mariachi music, and compose daily.

Miguel Martínez (second from left with trumpet) with his group Mariachi Tolteca. Private collection of Patricia Greathouse.

Jesús Rodríguez de Híjar, Mexico City, 2006. Photo © 2009 Christopher Barnes.

JESÚS RODRÍGUEZ DE HÍJAR

BORN JULY 10, 1929, TEQUILA, JALISCO, MEXICO

Affectionately known as *La Hormiga* (The Ant), Jesús Rodríguez de Híjar became a violinist with Mariachi Vargas de Tecalitlán in the mid-1950s. As their director and music arranger for over twenty years, he worked as Rubén Fuentes's right-hand man. Now, as director of Mariachi de América, he heads a top international group. Rodríguez de Híjar also devotes a great deal of time to mariachi education, both in Mexico and in the United States. As one of the organizers of Guadalajara's Encuentro Internacional del Mariachi y la Charrería, Rodríguez de Híjar has been instrumental in developing a mariachi conference in Mexico somewhat like those he has been part of in the United States.

Rodríguez de Híjar began playing the vihuela when he was six years old with his uncle, who played with Mariachi Tapatío de José Marmolejo. By the age of fourteen, he was studying classical violin technique under scholarship in Guadalajara. His father worked as a musician in an orchestra in Guadalajara, and young Jesús followed the family tradition. To him, mariachi was a musical career like any other. He says that being a mariachi musician is just a specialization for someone who has been well trained, similar to choosing to be a pediatrician after studying medicine. However, he emphasizes that any musician who is well trained and wants to play mariachi needs to learn the specific style.

After working in many excellent groups, Rodríguez de Híjar achieved his life's goal of playing in Mariachi Vargas. When he joined the group, they played mainly sones. He approached leader Silvestre Vargas, and told him that the mariachi needed to play all kinds of music. Vargas answered, "No, mariachis should play only our music."

Shortly thereafter, Rodríguez de Híjar succeeded Fuentes as music director of Mariachi Vargas. Under his guidance, Mariachi Vargas began playing pieces that were more romantic and more refined: "I spoke to the musicians in the group, and I explained to them that sones are played one way, and boleros are played another way—lightly and softly. Vargas was always cut and dried, 'Let's play "La Negra" top to bottom and—boom—let's go!'" Rodríguez de Híjar continues:

Apart from the music, I changed something very important as musical director of Mariachi Vargas. I decided that we were not going to accompany singers [from outside the group] anymore. It's hard work for a mariachi to accompany singers: the singer wants a song the mariachi doesn't know, and it takes a while to learn the basics of the song. Then the group has to deal with the interpretation, the key, note changes; it takes a long time to meld with the singer.

I bring young men into Mariachi de América between the ages of sixteen and twenty-five. For mariachi music, you need the strength of youth; a forty-year-old doesn't have the gusto, the life force to do it. I work with my group, performing with them on the stage, and I am dependent on them playing well. I would like to play as they do, but I don't have the strength and the spirit.

My goal is to see that people play mariachi music well.

RUBÉN FUENTES

BORN FEBRUARY 15, 1926, CIUDAD GUZMÁN, JALISCO, MEXICO

Rubén Fuentes is the man most responsible for the musical direction of the modern mariachi. Musical director of Mariachi Vargas after Silvestre Vargas, arranger for José Alfredo Jiménez, and president of RCA Victor in Mexico, his influence was and still is widespread. He advanced the careers and improved the musical style of many influential groups and artists through his vision and arrangements, and his taste and vision moved mariachi into the modern era. Every mariachi player in the world knows the mariachi national anthem, "Son de La Negra," one of many traditional pieces arranged by Fuentes. Today he continues to act as a musical entrepreneur, as well as owner and general director of Mariachi Vargas de Tecalitlán.

Mariachi Vargas, mid-1940s. Rubén Fuentes, second from left, top. Private collection of Patricia Greathouse.

Fuentes was unique when he joined Mariachi Vargas de Tecalitlán in 1944 as a young, classically trained violinist. Few, if any, formally educated violinists chose to play mariachi at that time. His musical training and natural ability served him well in his early years, and he became the musical director of RCA Records in Mexico during the mid-1950s. Fuentes was responsible not only for refining the sound of Mariachi Vargas but also for guiding them through a time of great productivity and setting the course for modern mariachi for over a half a century. Many pieces that form the basis of the mariachi repertoire are Fuentes's arrangements based on traditional music. A talented arranger, his pieces not only reflected regional roots, they increased the technical requirements for musicians. His arrangements brought complexity, drama, and dynamics to mariachi music.

Under Fuentes, music that had formerly been played in first position on the violin took advantage of the higher positions. (The standard untrained violin hand position is illustrated by Heriberto Molina on page 62. It prevents a violinist from playing in any position except first, which is the reason that experts bemoan the lack of good technique some student players display.)

Fuentes brought instruments into the recording studio that seldom had been used in modern mariachi recordings, writing parts for flutes, drums, organs, and orchestra. Under Fuentes, mariachi music also took a slight turn toward classical orchestral technique, using tremolo in the violins to create a shimmery atmosphere or to create tension.

NATI CANO

Born 1933, Ahuisculco, Jalisco, Mexico

Natividad Cano was born in Jalisco but moved to the United States as a young man. A leader in bringing mariachi music into the mainstream in the United States, he also reshaped the way mariachis view themselves by creating a permanent venue for his group, Los Camperos. Cano has also taken an active part in the mariachi education movement in the United States.

The son and grandson of musicians, Cano trained in classical violin at the Academia de Música in Guadalajara. As a child, he felt shame following his father and grandfather around the bars, asking for money from patrons as the band worked al talón. As an adult, he performed in the finest theaters in the world.

Cano worked his way up through groups, arriving in Los Angeles in 1959. There, he was hired to play in the house band, Mariachi Águila, at the Million Dollar Theater. In concerts, as in the movies, mariachis always backed singers, and the theater featured stars like José Alfredo Jiménez, Miguel Aceves Mejía, Javier Solís, Lola Beltrán, and Antonio Aguilar (who brought his horses onstage).

In most ways, the setting was the fulfillment of Cano's dream. He held a vision of a well-dressed mariachi performing a program of well-prepared music in concert to an attentive audience. When he became director of Mariachi Águila in 1961, he renamed them Los Camperos. As director, Cano rehearsed his group three to four hours a day and added gestures and movement to the group's performance. Cano was a strict disciplinarian who fired players who were lazy, missed practice, or drank too much, and he had his pick of ambitious and talented young Mexican musicians who wanted to work in the United States. In spite of his success, Cano wanted his mariachi group to be the main show, not a backup group. On tour with Miguel Aceves Mejía, Cano and some of his players were denied

Nati Cano, Teatro Degollado, Guadalajara, 2007. Photo © 2009 Jasper Schriber.

service at a restaurant in Texas—the establishment didn't serve Mexicans—and the experience reopened the old shame that Cano had suffered in his childhood. The experience inspired a restaurant that would serve everyone, with Los Camperos starring in a dinner show. La Fonda de los Camperos opened in Los Angeles in 1969.

Los Camperos de Nati Cano recorded with Linda Ronstadt and toured with her on her *Más Canciones* (More Songs) tour. They made historic recordings for the Smithsonian's Folkways program and continue as a magnet for talented young Mexican mariachis, although the original La Fonda has closed. Cano continues to perform and tour with Los Camperos; they are an important part of the Encuentro del Mariachi concerts in Guadalajara's Teatro Degollado.

RIGOBERTO ALFARO

Born 1934, Yurécuaro, Michoacán, Mexico

Rigoberto Alfaro is known as a talented arranger and producer and as one of the best guitar players in the history of mariachi. He was a part of Mariachi Vargas's dynamic armonía section during the golden age, and he appears on many classic mariachi recordings made during that period.

The son of a mariachi, Alfaro always loved the sound of strings. The guitar particularly attracted him; as a small boy, he would pluck the strings and say wistfully, *"¡Qué bonita! (How pretty!)"* One day, his father brought home a guitar for safekeeping that belonged to a fellow musician. The temptation was too much for young Alfaro, and he played the guitar behind his father's back, knowing it was against his wishes. When Alfaro's father found that his son had been playing the guitar, he said, "If you want to be a musician, you'll have to take lessons so you will be a good player!"

When the family moved to Nuevo Laredo, Mexico, the nine-year-old could play only three chords on the guitar, but his father, the leader of a mariachi, asked him to join his group. According to Alfaro, the players were very humble and modest and didn't make a great sound. It was rare that he was paid for his work, but it was the beginning of a career. A year later, the family moved to Mexico City. Alfaro's father worked hard to support eight children, and he hoped the city would be a place where he could get ahead. Alfaro had never had a teacher, but once in the city he found La Escuela Libre de Música y Declamación (The Free School of Music and Elocution). The school didn't teach mariachi music. José E. Vazquez, a member of the symphony, ran it and taught the history of music, musical dictation, note reading, arranging, and solfège (a method for sight singing and note reading based on do, re, mi, fa, so, la, ti).

The Alfaro family still struggled in the city, and young Alfaro had to contribute to help the family survive. By his late teens, he had left his father's mariachi to join better groups. Playing until 5:00 or 6:00 in the morning, he would sleep in a church for a few hours then get up for his first music class at 8:00.

Fortunate in the ability to recall everything he heard, Alfaro began writing out arrangements of the popular music from the radio. His new group became more successful and made more money by playing the latest songs.

When Alfaro was twenty-five years old, he was invited to join Mariachi Vargas. For a young man who loved music, it was an important step. People noticed his musical ability, and he made a name for himself.

In 1970, Alfaro received an offer to work in the recording industry. He had to decide whether to leave what he calls "the best group ever" or to stay with Vargas and lose an opportunity to advance his career. Luckily, Jesús Rodríguez de Híjar, director of Mariachi Vargas, made the decision easier, saying, "Go, give it a try! If it doesn't work out, you can always come back."

With that in mind, Alfaro left Mariachi Vargas. He became an outstanding arranger of ranchera music, a record producer, and the musical director of one of Mexico's most popular TV programs, *Siempre en Domingo (Always on Sunday)*.

Although he no longer performs, Alfaro still works as an arranger and producer and frequently travels to the United States to teach in conferences, joining his old colleagues and delighting his students.

Rigoberto Alfaro, Los Angeles, California, 2008.
Photo © 2009 Christopher Barnes.

HERIBERTO MOLINA

Born December 4, 1930, Ixelajuacan del Río, Jalisco, Mexico

Heriberto Molina's nickname is *La Cura* (The Priest), as he studied for the priesthood before becoming a lead singer and violinist with Mariachi Vargas. On many recordings his resonant, rich voice is a splendid example of what a mariachi singer can be with taste, training, and discipline.

When he was three, Heriberto Molina sang his first song, one called *"Tus Pupilas Eran de Fuego* (Your Eyes Were Aflame)," a rather sophisticated number for someone barely out of diapers. His father was a musical director and rehearsed his orchestra in the family home. Little Heriberto was totally immersed in music and wanted to be a musician above all else.

By six, he had already learned to play trumpet and was part of the town band.

But in spite of following his dream of being a musician, Molina went to work in a bank. In a restaurant with friends one day, he sang a song with the mariachi, and a customer tipped him. Looking at the money, he was amazed to see that it was significantly more than the wages he made in a week at the bank. He decided that mariachi was a career that held some promise.

To refine his vocal technique, Molina studied with Noé Quintero, the teacher of Pedro Infante and Javier Solís. After many years with Vargas, he immigrated to the United States. His doctor told him that he would live much longer at low altitude because of his heart problems.

As one of the foremost vocal coaches in California, Molina has reached the stage where he is impatient with sloppy musicians, and knows how things could be better. He says that mariachi violin teachers in the United States "don't teach the correct hand position, and they don't teach children to play in tune!" He also says, "Rhythm and meter are brothers. Poor rhythm is often a defect of singers. More than anything else, singers should learn to play instruments so they will be musicians!"

Molina sees a brighter future for mariachi music in the United States than in Mexico. However, he says that one drawback is the lack of authentic mariachis to teach in the states. He gets exasperated that teachers of other music genres, such as jazz and classical, think they can teach mariachi without any mariachi training.

Now retired from performance, Molina maintains a studio in his home where he works with students, including top up-and-coming Latino stars. He is also a popular teacher at conferences across the United States.

Heriberto Molina demonstrates incorrect violin hand position, Pico Rivera, California, 2008. Photo © 2009 Christopher Barnes.

MAKING A LIVING

Mariachis are modern troubadours; they play in many different kinds of settings, ranging from intimate face-to-face serenades to television. Performance venues correspond in great part to the skill, the luck, and the status of a given group.

AL TALÓN

In Querétaro, a modern troubadour waits for work on a rainy night. Photo credit © 2008 Ivan Guerrero Guevara. BELOW: Mariachis in Mexico City. Photo © 2009 Madeleine de Sinety.

When mariachis stroll from table to table in a restaurant or bar offering to play songs for a price, they are working al talón (literally, on the heel). Also called "the kitty," it's the most common and also the most difficult way for mariachis to earn money. The patron pays, and the mariachi plays; they're a live jukebox. It's the least artistically satisfying way to make a living, but almost every mariachi musician, no matter how grand, has worked al talón at one time or another.

Tlaquepaque, a charming town of shops and artisans within the Guadalajara metropolis, is the site of the famous El Parian, home to numerous roaming mariachi groups. It's one of the most well-known plazas in Mexico for mariachi music, and one always finds groups for hire there. Mariachis circulate through the open air restaurants that ring the square, and on special occasions, there are amplified mariachis on the bandstand.

On Sundays, El Parian fills ups with a street market and food vendors serving favorites like tortas ahogadas (smothered sandwiches), a Guadalajara specialty. Families cruise for ice cream, cotton candy, hot dogs, hamburgers, or grilled corn either on a stick or cut from the cob and served in cups with mayonnaise. Street musicians vie for customers, and in the early evenings, mariachis come out to work al talón.

To get an idea of how it might be to work al talón, imagine, whatever your job, that you and your colleagues are required as a group to give a short presentation from memory on the spur of the moment about anything you or anyone else has ever learned about your field. That's the position of mariachis performing al talón. The patron requests a song—an old family favorite from an obscure 78 rpm recording that belonged to his or her grandma or the hottest new song from a Tex-Mex pop star—and expects the mariachi to know it. Mariachis generally have a repertoire of over two thousand songs, and will try to find a way to satisfy a request. Even if only a

Elotes Asados

(Mexican-Style Grilled Corn)

The corn grilled and sold on street corners in Mexico is sturdier and starchier than sweet corn in the United States, but any corn is delicious cooked this way. Those who may look askance at putting mayonnaise and chile on

corn will be turned into believers with the first bite. Grilled corn is great with any kind of barbecued meats or fish, but we particularly like it with the Mexican Dip Sandwich.

Serves 4

6 heavy-duty wooden skewers, soaked for an hour
6 ears of fresh sweet corn, shucked
Olive or vegetable oil
Mayonnaise
Finely grated queso añejo or Parmesan cheese
Chile powder (use singly or in combination from
   the following list:
Ground pure New Mexico red chile powder,
   ground chile pequin, Aleppo pepper flakes,
   ancho chile powder)

Lime sections
Large grain (kosher or Maldon) salt and freshly
   ground pepper, to taste

Heat up a gas fire or charcoal grill. Firmly stick a soaked wooden skewer in the stem end of the corn, then roll the ears of corn in oil. Grill the corn over a medium-hot fire until it is toasted golden and brown in spots, 10–12 minutes total.

Slather corn all over with mayonnaise, sprinkle with cheese, and dust with chile powder. Serve with lime sections and salt and pepper on the side.

Mariachi Águila violinists, Tlaquepaque, Mexico.
Photo © Patricia Greathouse.

couple of group members know the song, they'll play it. Knowledge of generic beginnings and endings, stock adornos (embellishments), and rhythm patterns in the armonía help flesh out the performance.

When a mariachi is playing al talón, the physical closeness between the musicians and the customers increases intimacy but can also cause deep discomfort. Musicians are their own managers, negotiating with customers about prices and requests. Patrons who are prepared to spend a lot of money are easy for mariachis to spot and may be the main source of revenue for the group on any given day.

Mark Fogelquist tells the story of Mariachi Internacional of Tijuana entertaining a customer from 1:00 p.m. until 10:00 p.m., when they stopped and another mariachi played until midnight. The trumpet player launched into song after song without pausing, and the group was able to bill the customer for 240 songs in nine hours—twenty-six songs an hour! (The normal rate of play is about twenty

songs an hour.) In addition, the customer bought thirteen rounds of drinks for the mariachis to "keep them primed."

The amount a group can make in a day varies wildly, from zero on a slow day to several hundred dollars on a great day. Compared to the daily wage in Mexico, which is between five and seven U.S. dollars, mariachis make good money, especially for young men who also like the lifestyle and perks. It's far more enjoyable and cleaner than manual labor. For patrons, there's nothing like enjoying a cold drink on a beautiful patio, serenaded by the sound of live music. However, mariachis are at the mercy of any patron with enough money to hire the group. A mean-tempered or drunk patron can make things difficult. Nati Cano, the leader of Mariachi Los Camperos, has compared working al talón to prostitution. Some groups charge a great deal more than the going rate of about three U.S. dollars a song in Mexico, but the situation of temporary indentured servitude is the same, regardless of the price.

CHAMBA

A chamba (gig) can be scheduled in advance, contracted for, or even arranged on the spur of the moment. Mariachis hang out in centers like Plaza Garibaldi in Mexico City, La Plaza de Mariachis in Guadalajara, or the Mariachi Plaza de Los Angeles, California, waiting for work, and negotiate rates on the spot. They then jump into a car and follow the patron to the chamba. The mariachi performs wherever the patron wishes, from a backyard to the governor's mansion. Rates are agreed upon ahead of time, and charges are by the hour. These days, the going rate for a local mariachi in the United States (even a student mariachi) can range from $250 to $500 an hour, depending on the skill and prestige of the group. Top mariachis make much more than that and can often command per diem fees and travel expenses as well.

The perks of playing a chamba for a wealthy patron can be rewarding. Mariachi Tenampa of Albuquerque, New Mexico, was once hired to play a housewarming party on the Greek island of Mykonos. They were paid well for their four performances, and the all-expense-paid ten-day trip also included sailing, swimming, and

Bizarre scenes have awaited mariachis, according to Jonathan Clark. Clark knew of a mariachi that was hired by some narcotraficantes (drug dealers) and paid double to play for an orgy—the only requirement was that they play dressed only in moños (neckties) and boots. They were happy for the job, as they hadn't had any work in three days and were starving.

Clark also relates a story about mariachis hired by narcotraficantes to play for a party; after awhile, the patrons asked the musicians to play standing in the swimming pool. The mariachis protested that it would ruin their instruments and trajes, and the drug dealers pulled out a wad of bills and said, "We'll pay for new trajes and instruments! Get in the pool!"

Mariachis play cards to kill time until they get hired. Photo © 2009 Jasper Schriber.

A warm-up during a shoe shine. Photo © 2009 Christopher Barnes.

Veteran mariachis negotiate a job on Plaza Garibaldi, New Year's Day, 2007. Photo © 2009 Madeleine de Sinety.

Wedding chamba.
Photo © 2009
Christopher Barnes.

A trumpeter warms up
while waiting for work,
Plaza Garibaldi.
Photo © 2009
Madeleine de Sinety.

ABOVE: *A mariachi performs for a wedding, Tepozotlán, Mexico, 2007. Photo © 2009 Christopher Barnes. FACING: Mariachi Azteca. Left to right: Fernando Romero, Rachel Miller, Christina Gomez, Eddie Hernández. Photo © 2009 Christopher Barnes.*

generally joining in all of the other festivities offered by their generous patron.

However, most mariachis don't know exactly what they'll find when they accept a chamba—they may be asked to play outside in freezing, sleeting weather, or inside a beautiful house with an attentive audience in a concert setting. Parties can be lively and fun to play, with everyone joining in and dancing, or they can be dead, with guests acting as if the mariachi were audible wallpaper.

My mariachi, Mariachi Azteca of Santa Fe, New Mexico, was once asked to play in a separate room because we were too loud, so we had a good time playing for each other and making jokes out of sight of the guests. Some hosts are proud to have mariachis in their homes and treat them like guests: chatting, hugging, bringing drinks, and inviting them to eat. Others forget to offer any food or drink at all or ask that the mariachis eat in the kitchen and arrive and depart via the back door.

Luckily for most mariachis, those types of chambas are anomalies; most chambas involve playing for celebrations and parties at family homes or rented halls. At fiestas in Mexico and for Mexican families living in the United

States, dancing is part of the festivities. Cumbias are favorites, and many people have learned folkloric dance as part of school curricula and programs throughout Mexico and the southwestern part of the United States. When sones start, there are always a few people who will wow the crowd by dancing the zapateada, the foot-stomping moves that traditionally go with the son.

When the mariachis, tequila, and beer have cast their spell, someone inevitably asks the mariachis to accompany them in a song. An experienced group can find the correct key and help along the most tin-eared, rhythm-challenged

All families have treasured songs that they request, sometimes in advance so the mariachi can make sure to play them at the party. Our group once played "Volver, Volver" for a family whose father had died many years before. They still missed him and "Volver, Volver" had been his favorite song. The children placed a chair for their mother in front of the mariachi, and they all stood around her, holding her hands while we played the song and she cried.

Mariachi Azteca serenades customers at a Sunday brunch in a restaurant in Santa Fe, New Mexico. Left to right: Audrey Davis, Patricia Greathouse, Gary Gonzales, Fernando Romero, Eddie Hernández. Photo © Christopher Barnes.

singer, who invariably is cheered on by friends and family. Occasionally, a true talent or professional singer will ask to sing with the group.

Sometimes a mariachi will play for a fiesta; it's a wonderful feeling to play beloved music and to see the spirit of alegría (joy) that a mariachi adds to a party. On one memorable occasion, established middle-aged newlyweds invited the whole rural village to the groom's ancestral adobe home. They danced to every song we played, and soon everyone—children, grandmothers, and neighbors—was on the dance floor, laughing, singing, waving their arms, and cheering for the mariachi. They brought us food and drinks so we wouldn't stop the music. We played on and on, hour after hour, and the party crescendoed until everyone finally quit in exhaustion. It was a great party, and I can't think of better fun than to play to such an appreciative audience.

SERENATA

Mariachis may play serenatas in the middle of the night, at dawn, or at any other time the customer wants to serenade a loved one. In the old days, when young Mexican ladies were carefully guarded by chaperones, young men

LEFT: Woman singing in El Numero 1, Mexico City. Photo © 2009 Madeleine de Sinety. ABOVE: A violinist performs at La Ribera in Mexico City. Photo © 2009 Madeleine de Sinety. BELOW: Singing along in Tepozotlán. Photo © 2009 Christopher Barnes.

had a difficult time speaking to the women they admired; instead, they hired mariachis to serenade their beloved outside the window. Passionate songs were a good way to convey the message of love and longing.

Nowadays, people still hire mariachis to express their sentiments to people they love—husbands in disfavor with their wives may hire a mariachi to gain forgiveness, and adult children hire mariachis to play "Las Mañanitas" to thrill Mom on Mother's Day or her birthday. In fact, "Las Mañanitas" may be the single most useful song in the mariachi repertoire; it's played for every occasion requiring congratulations or celebration.

THE PLANTA

The planta is a regular job for a mariachi, usually in a hotel, nightclub, or restaurant, but it could also be in an amusement park or on a cruise ship. Very few groups are as fortunate as Mariachi Cobre, who has worked for Disney at EPCOT Center for more than twenty-five years. They are well paid and receive benefits and financial security. For a planta, most businesses hire mariachis to play during defined hours on regular days. They are free to work outside that time, playing private engagements or conducting other business. In the United States, restaurants usually

ABOVE: A singer performs at El Numero 1 in Mexico City. Photo © 2009 Madeleine de Sinety. RIGHT: The joy of being backed up by a professional mariachi, Mexico City, 2006. Photo © 2009 Madeleine de Sinety.

hire mariachis for peak hours; they may play a set, take a break, and return to stroll from table to table for a second hour. The restaurant will pay a lower hourly rate than the mariachi is usually paid because of the regularity of the work and the possibility of tips.

In Mexico City, two restaurants across the street from each other offer typical Mexican food and excellent mariachi music; La Ribera and El Numero 1 compete for customers in safe, well-lit settings.

In Mexico, it's common for restaurants to schedule mariachis, require them to be present for certain hours, and not guarantee them any pay—they must rely on tips for their income, which can vary wildly depending on the season, the weather, the day of the week, and the customer who walks in the door. The hours can be excruciatingly long and filled with boredom if business is slow.

This rarely happens in the United States, where mariachis expect to be paid for showing up. In some restaurants, customers may consider music to be part of the cost of dinner; in other cases, customers may have come for the food and consider the music a vexation. In general, however, restaurants profit from hiring mariachis during the dinner hour; customers tend to order more drinks and food, and a popular mariachi will draw in their fans. A regular planta benefits mariachis, too, as prospective clients have a place to hear and see the group before hiring them, and the group can meet new customers for future chambas.

SHOWS

Shows are small concerts where the mariachi is the center of attraction; they control both the content and the timing of the presentation. Depending on the venue, a mariachi might work up to seven short shows a day, as Mariachi Cobre does at EPCOT Center.

The performers know exactly what pieces are on the program and almost never take requests; fans can expect to see flawless performances and excellent musicianship. The

ABOVE: Mariachi Tenampa rides a float at the Santa Fe Fiesta Historical/Hysterical Parade. Photo courtesy of José Santiago, New Mexico. FACING: Mariachi Azteca (in background) plays to Santa Fe Fiesta Court, New Mexico. Photo © 2009 Christopher Barnes.

show setting is sometimes not as lively as a cantina setting, where anything can happen and spontaneity is the rule of the day, but they are suitable family entertainment.

Sometimes dinner is served with the show. Nati Cano pioneered the concept at his La Fonda in Los Angeles, and now there are numerous restaurants and nightclubs in the United States and Mexico that showcase mariachis.

FESTIVALS AND FIESTAS

In both the United States and Mexico, local celebrations call for a performance stage where mariachis often alternate with other musical groups to provide continuous entertainment, filling several days with music. Groups

commonly play thirty minutes to an hour in these settings, and sometimes there is more than one stage. Performances are usually free or quite inexpensive, and music lovers bring blankets or folding chairs and spend the afternoon enjoying the music, eating, and socializing. Community festivals and fiestas often provide mariachis with a chance to make a lot of money in a concentrated week of work.

The Santa Fe Fiesta, culminating the weekend after Labor Day, celebrates the "bloodless" reconquest of the ancient capital of New Spain in New Mexico. The oldest community celebration in the United States, it's full of pageantry, food, and mariachi music. Mariachis play on the plaza, make rounds on a chartered bus with fiesta royalty, and visit schools, nursing homes, private businesses, and government offices to generate excitement and inspire the community to join in the celebrations. Preparations take

all year, during which the Fiesta Council chooses a queen and her court of princesas. A local man plays Don Diego de Vargas, the leader of the Spanish soldiers, and his band of men take the parts of the mayor, soldiers, friars, and even a bugle boy.

The Santa Fe Fiesta Council contracts with several different mariachis—from school groups to top performers—to meet the exhausting demands of the stage performances, coronation, visitations, official dances, masses, parades, and concerts that take place during the two weeks leading up to the Santa Fe Fiesta. Mariachis accompany La Conquistadora, an image of the Virgin, as the devoted carry her from the cathedral to a small chapel, as well as play for the annual procession from the cathedral to the Cross of the Martyrs.

CONFERENCES

One of the ways that professional mariachis diversify their work and pass on their knowledge is teaching at student workshops as part of mariachi conferences (page 132). A phenomenon that began in the United States in the 1970s, *encuentros* (meetings) and conferences are now also a part of Mexican mariachi culture. For many excellent mariachis, the opportunity to teach in conferences has added an exciting dimension to their profession, giving them the opportunity to pass on skills, mentor students, socialize with colleagues from other groups, write new arrangements, and earn money without having to put on a traje.

Mack Ruiz, Israel Molina, and Hector Gama of Mariachi Cobre teach a violin class at the San Jose Mariachi Conference, 2007. Photo © 2009 Christopher Barnes.

Mariachi Vargas onstage at Teatro Degollado with La Orquesta Filarmonica de Jalisco, 2007 (left to right, Pepe Martínez Jr., Daniel Martínez, and Arturo Vargas). Photo © 2009 Jasper Schriber.

CONCERTS AND SYMPHONIC APPEARANCES

Most mariachis don't tour and play in large concert venues unless they are accompanying a headlining soloist or are participating in a festival or conference. However, within the last thirty years, symphony orchestras have begun to offer top mariachis an opportunity to play in pop concerts to people who may never have heard a mariachi. Each group has its own musical arrangements and provides them to the host orchestra. Groups like Mariachi Vargas de Tecalitlán, Mariachi Cobre, Mariachi Sol de Mexico, and Mariachi los Camperos have all played with symphony orchestras. During the Encuentro Internacional del Mariachi y la Charrería in Guadalajara, there are five straight sold-out nights of concerts at the Teatro Degollado that include mariachis and La Orquesta Filarmonica de Jalisco.

MARIACHI MASS

With the inclusion of folk music in the liturgy of churches in the United States, a new arena opened for mariachis as well. In 1966, the first mariachi mass, Misa Panamericana, was performed at a small chapel in Cuernavaca, Mexico. The popularity of the mass spread so quickly that it is now performed regularly in the cathedral of the same church. Mariachi masses are played throughout the United States too. They're popular for weddings, baptisms, funerals, and especially on December 12 for the Virgin of Guadalupe's saint's day. For weddings, mariachis play outside the church to welcome guests; after the service, they often lead the wedding party outside and play as the guests leave the church.

LA CANTINA

Most cantinas are places where working people can drop the mask of deference and express true emotions. Patrons find alegría, relief from the pressures of life, and a safe place to cry. Music and alcohol provide inhibition-lowering nudges, and few people in the world celebrate with the intensity and drama of Mexicans—tears are as plentiful as laughter at fiestas. The cantina is a never-ending fiesta, but there's a dangerous edge. Violence is just under the surface, and passion is the spark that ignites the tinder of alcohol and suppressed emotion. Mariachi music is the sound track, an intrinsic part of the draw of cantinas. Important sources of revenue for mariachis, cantinas enable many to earn their livings.

My cantina tutorial happened one steamy afternoon on the most southerly dip of the coast of Mexico near Tehuantepec. During an afternoon of driving—thirsty from the long hot road—my husband at the time stopped at a benign-looking cantina on the side of the road in a little port town called Salina Cruz. Hearing boisterous laughter and music, we opened the door; sound and motion stopped, and everyone turned our way. Flies wafted deafeningly through the air. The faces were all male. I stepped over the threshold, heat and thirst mudding my good judgment. A man seated next to the door appraised me from head to foot—disbelief, amusement, and challenge on his face. Finally, someone broke the tension with a low whistle and a slow headshake, as if telling an unbelievable story. They threw chuckles, hoots, and comments at our backs as we turned and headed back into the glaring sunlight. There are some cantinas in Mexico that respectable women just don't enter.

The cantina is the perfect place for courtship, heartbreak, and vengeance. Love in all its manifestations is the essence of the mariachi repertoire. Countless sorrowful songs like *"Los Laureles"* (The Bay Trees) tell of betrayal by heartless, deceitful lovers: *"La perdición de los hombres son las malditas mujeres* (The ruin of men is wicked women).*"

Other songs are lighthearted and full of good eye-winking fun. For a few dollars, a patron can hire a group to play the background music to the current episode in his or her life.

THE PANACEA OF THE CANTINA

Modern mariachi music is full of references to the power of alcohol, none more so than the music of José Alfredo Jiménez. While life may not be worthless, as he says in *"Camino de Guanajuato,"* it does seem to be incredibly cheap. For certain occasions, the fiesta—and ritual drinking—is the rule of the day. People party as if their lives depended on it. Even in upper-class families, young men are expected to sow wild oats, and mariachis have long been an important part of the festivities.

The corrido "La Rafaelita," written by Miguel Martínez, tells the story of two friends who begin drinking in a cantina, and in the course of the afternoon wind up crossing the river to shoot it out over a woman named Raphaelita. The young men kill each other, and the ending, as with most corridos, offers a moral: *"Por una mancornadora murieron dos gallos finos* (Because of a cheating woman, two fine roosters died).*"

THE QUEEN OF CANTINAS

Salón Tenampa is the most famous cantina in all of Mexico, responsible for making the Plaza Garibaldi the world center of mariachi. Without Juan Indalecio Hernández Ibarra's bar that gathered the people and spirit of Jalisco to the site, who knows where mariachi groups would have congregated? Originally from Cocula, Hernández began Tenampa on Honduras Street in 1923 on one side of Plaza Garibaldi. He attracted his countrymen by serving pomegranate and myrtle punch, a regional drink made by his wife, Amalia Díaz de Hernández. She also made delicious plates of typical Jaliscan food—birria, pozole, enchiladas, and tacos. But most importantly to the future of Garibaldi, Hernández offered live mariachi music.

The first group to play at Garibaldi was Concho Andrade's mariachi. Andrade was an associate of Hernández from Cocula. During the time Andrade's group was beginning the tradition of mariachis in Garibaldi, the Cristero Rebellion broke out, violently threatening the people of Jalisco. Andrade's mariachis had to choose between staying in the city and making money and going home to try to protect their families.

The most venerable cantina on Plaza Garibaldi, the Salón Tenampa is still a vibrant working bar. The most famous names in Mexican music who performed there include but are not limited to Lola Beltrán, José Alfredo Jiménez, Vicente Fernández, Javier Solís, Miguel Aceves Mejía, Lucha Villa, Pedro Vargas, Agustín Lara, Jorge Negrete, Pedro Infante, and Amalia Mendoza, all accompanied by the best mariachi groups.

BAND BONDING

For modern mariachis, extensive travel is a necessary part of doing business. Whether by plane, bus, or car, travel is a good time to socialize and enjoy the companionship of

Tenampa, the first business to feature mariachis on Plaza Garibaldi, Mexico City.

Mariachi Nuevo Tecalitlán bus. Photo © 2009 Patricia Greathouse.

fellow mariachis. Some successful mariachis even have their own buses, emblazoned with their names and pictures on the side.

In my time as a violinist with Mariachi Azteca, I became accustomed to traveling in a van with my colleagues. We caught up on the news, talked politics, and teased each other mercilessly. We called it "band bonding."

During the Encuentro Internacional del Mariachi y la Charrería held in Guadalajara, I had the great pleasure of traveling along on buses with three different Mexican mariachis to concerts in outlying areas, and I discovered that band bonding is a universal rite.

BUS RIDE TO THE COAST

The first trip was to Tecomán, Colima, on the Pacific coast of Mexico. I took a frantic taxi across Guadalajara to be on the bus at two in the afternoon, as instructed.

About four thirty, a single mariachi turned up, smiling and carrying his traje in a suit bag in one hand and a plastic container in the other. He introduced himself as Sabas López and sat down on the seat next to me. He told me he played violin with Mariachi Sol de América.

Soon, mariachis were streaming onto the bus, and the air was charged with the excitement of going on a gig. Young women from Mariachi Femenil Nuevo Tecalitlán were getting on the bus, too, looking like models boarding a plane on the way to the runway in Milan, their makeup kits in hand.

Sabas passed around his container of pineapple and papaya in lime juice and chile.

Sabas started his musical training at sixteen with a well-known teacher. He had to sell fruit to help his mother support the family and to earn money to pay for his lessons. "Here in Mexico, things are different than in the

United States," he told me; it is a common refrain among the mariachis I talk to. There's no state or educational support for learning to be a mariachi. His teacher trained him in the traditional classical manner—solfège, note reading, and musical transcription in addition to violin.

Although the scenic countryside southeast of Guadalajara—green pastures with mountains in the background—is beautiful and interesting to tourists, the mariachis were soon restless, and eventually boredom set in, which meant the teasing would begin.

I moved over to sit with Lalo, one of the two directors of Mariachi Sol de América. Sabas protested. Lalo put his arm around me. If I hadn't been desensitized by years of relentless teasing by the Mariachi Azteca men, I would have been embarrassed, but I knew this was about relieving boredom and having a little fun.

 # Ensalada de Frutas

(Mexican Fruit Salad)

One of the most common Mexican street foods, fruit in cups or on a stick is sold by vendors wielding knives with the grace of Japanese chefs. Use Ataulfo mangoes if you can find them—their spicy sweet, slightly acidic flavor is perfect. When serving this salad, invite guests to add more lime juice and to sprinkle chile powder and salt on top—it's an amazing combination; the chile and salt intensify the flavors of the fruit.

> 1 pound ripe yellow Ataulfo mangoes (about 2), peeled and cubed
> 1 pound fresh pineapple, peeled and cut in small chunks
> 1 pound ripe cantaloupe or papaya, peeled and cut in small chunks
> 1/2 cup freshly squeezed orange juice (about 2 oranges)
> 2 tablespoons freshly squeezed lime juice
> Coarse salt
> Chile flakes
> Lime wedges

Combine the fruit and juices in a bowl. Mix gently and serve immediately or cover and refrigerate several hours. Serve with the condiments on the side.

Photo © 2009 Christopher Barnes.

Gerardo-of-the-faces cures boredom on a bus ride to the coast, 2007. Photo © 2009 Patricia Greathouse.

Lalo began to compliment me with wild hyperbole, almost reflexively, and I thanked him. I told him how much easier it was for me to travel in Mexico now that I'm a grandmother and don't have long blonde hair. He protested guilelessly—"But why?"

Eventually, I told him about how things are different in the United States; unlike in Mexico, men rarely call out to pretty girls on the street, calling them fresca and muñeca (strawberry and doll). Women move about more freely.

Several of the band members were leaning in, listening carefully now.

"You mean in the United States men don't compliment women?" Lalo asked.

I said, "Yes, they do, but usually face to face, after they've met, or privately when they're close."

They were amazed, stunned. "What's wrong with American men? Don't they like women? And the women, they like it this way?"

(It was interesting to me that the men didn't approach the beautiful young women mariachis on the bus, who were traveling with their chaperone.)

Mariachi Sol de América has seen most of the United States, Europe, Latin America, and Japan. They try to incorporate their vacations into their performance travel. And, no, their wives and families have never gone with them.

Sabas made a fuss about me moving back to sit with him, but by that time, Lalo was playing with my camera, taking pictures of Gerardo, the guitarist. Gerardo made faces and then looked at them and commented on how handsome he was. The rest of the men were hooting and hollering and naming his faces—"Mad dog!" "Crybaby!" "Baboon!"

He had a plastic face and was insistent that Lalo catch every grimace on the camera.

The other mariachis started talking and singing in baby voices; the country we were passing through had changed from verdant fields to rocky mountains cut by deep gorges and wild rivers. The two-lane concrete bridges were narrow, the bus was wide, the chasms deep. Octavio cried out in his baby voice for his mother.

ARRIVAL IN TECOMÁN

It was drizzling, but the men piled off the bus to meet and shake hands with Mariachi Nuevo Tecalitlán. Showing respect and admiration for other groups is a normal part of mariachi culture. The unspoken rule is: Never speak badly of other mariachis, never show your envy or competitiveness, always support and compliment others' performances. It is a legacy based on common sense; you might someday want to work in that other group, or you might want them to work in yours.

I got off the bus, too, glad to stand. Gerardo approached me, and with a serious face told me that I was a beautiful woman. I searched his face, now composed and untelling, for a clue. Did he mean beautiful in the same way that he was a handsome man? I demurred, and he persisted; he was a red-blooded Mexican man, after all, and I was a woman with a pulse. It reminded me of the refrain to the song "Yo el Aventurero (I, the Adventurer)":

Me gustan . . .
Las altas y las chaparritas,
Las flacas, las gordas y las chiquititas,
Solteras y viudas y divorciaditas,
Me encantan las chatas de caras bonitas; . . .
Me encantan las gordas retejaladoras
Que tengan hermanos que no sean celosos,
Que tengan sus novios caras de babosos,
Me encanta la vida, me gusta el amor,
Soy aventurero revacilador.

I like . . .
The tall ones and the short ones,
The skinny ones, the fat ones and the small ones,
The single ones, the widows and the divorcées,
I love the girlfriends with the pretty faces. . . .
I love the agreeable chubby ones
That may have brothers that aren't jealous,
That may have boyfriends that slobber,
I love life, I love love,
I'm a fickle adventurer.

Getting ready to go onstage.
Photo © 2009 Patricia
Greathouse.

The women stayed on the bus to put on their makeup. A cyan half-moon, painted on each eye to the arch under the brow, was standard. Their hair, pulled back straight into a low ponytail, was topped with a net and satin bow. They were making the transition to divas.

BACKSTAGE

The community center in Tecomán was set up for feeding a crowd. There was a table well stocked with Fresca and Coca Cola; a keg of beer, bottles of tequila, and mineral water stood by. Tented areas with grills, long tables, and crates of plates promised a feast.

A stout gray-haired woman was half-bent, kneading a huge amount of masa in a blue plastic milk crate for home-made tortillas.

In their backstage room, Mariachi Sol de América was having a violin sectional practice. The women were changing into their trajes in their room.

Two angelic young men in light green trajes were in a room playing piano. They were part of Mariachi Santa Cecilia, the opening group. They take lessons at a music program at this very community center in both mariachi and classical music. José, the tall boy, his head full of black curls, gave me a wet buss on the cheek when we met. He is somebody's darling *jito* and has been brought up to treat old ladies with courtesy—no wincing! José plays violin in the local orchestra. He and his friend played Vivaldi when they got bored playing the piano.

Mariachi Santa Cecilia, Tecomán, Colima, Mexico. Photo © 2009 Patricia Greathouse.

Mariachi Femenil Nuevo Tecalitlán, Tecomán, Colima, 2007. Photo © 2009 Patricia Greathouse.

Mariachi Nuevo Tecalitlán, Tecomán, Colima, 2007. Photo © 2009 Patricia Greathouse.

THE CONCERT

The concert was supposed to start at nine in the evening, but there were only a few people waiting in the auditorium.

At ten, the auditorium was half full. At ten fifteen, Mariachi Santa Cecilia came onstage in a blaze of energy. They were fabulous performers—fresh and confident. The lead singer was a showman; when he smiled, his braces belied the maturity of his voice.

Mariachi Femenil Nuevo Tecalitlán took the stage. The women were sexy and glamorous—they engaged the audience and played beautifully. The intimacy of the experience was unique for a concert setting.

Next up was Mariachi Nuevo Tecalitlán. Their sound was huge—they had, in addition to a full complement of instruments, a harpist. The highlight of their show was the "Sarasate Zapateado" that two violinists—the Martínez brothers—played in concerto-duo form, trading off the solo parts. The mariachi played during the tutti passages, and the crowd went wild.

How could Mariachi Sol de América follow this? But they came on after midnight as if they were opening the show, fresh horses for a tired audience.

The first surprise was Octavio. His tenor was full and expressive, and he sang passionately with drama and conviction. His home was the stage; here he controlled the universe.

Armando Tinoco, the superbly accomplished requinto and guitarra de golpe player, stood on the end, stage right, unnoticeable except when it was his turn to lead. When he launched into *"Noches de Barcelona,"* he showed the

Octavio Irineo Maciel, Mariachi Sol de América, Tecomán, Colima, Mexico, 2007. Photo © 2009 Patricia Greathouse.

Armando Cervantes Tinoco plays a solo on the guitarra de golpe, Mariachi Sol de América, Tecomán, Colima, Mexico, 2007. Photo © 2009 Patricia Greathouse.

Gerardo Buenrostro Arias as Vicente Fernandez, Mariachi Sol de América, Tecomán, Colima, Mexico, 2007. Photo © 2009 Patricia Greathouse.

unique niche that Mariachi Sol de América holds in the Jalisco mariachi constellation. The piece rocked, complete with an atypical, complex, noodling solo riff that was at once totally rhythmical and totally improvisational in nature, displaying Armando's virtuosity. The call and response shape of the songs was both modern and classical. The crowd was frantic when he finished.

Gerardo-of-the-Faces put on his sombrero and came down on the floor, looking like a *patito feo* (ugly duckling) on the warpath. Or maybe a Mexican version of Yosemite Sam.

He did a send-up of Mexican ranchero star Vicente Fernández, singing a romantic ballad to an elderly woman with all the passion of a young man in love. I know now

that his earlier vignette with me was good practice for this performance. It was fascinating to watch him—a form of superb psychodrama on a subtle scale.

Sabas had disappeared from the violin section. He appeared at the back of the auditorium making a fuss, a red-and-white blanket folded over his shoulder and a half-empty bottle of tequila his hand.

He continued his noisy way down the center aisle, talking and carrying on. Along the way he stopped to pour tequila down the gullet of an audience member. The man tipped his head back, becoming an endless drain.

Sabas stopped to give a well-dressed middle-aged woman her turn. She had to pause and dry her face. Another grandmother came to the front to take the sacrament

Sabas López as José Alfredo, Mariachi Sol de América, Tecomán, Colima, Mexico, 2007. Photo © 2009 Patricia Greathouse.

Sabas López, Mariachi Sol de América, Tecomán, Colima, Mexico, 2007. Photo © 2009 Patricia Greathouse.

Sabas López, Mariachi Sol de América, Tecomán, Colima, Mexico, 2007. Photo © 2009 Patricia Greathouse.

Jalisco style, straight out of the bottle.

Sabas positioned himself between the rows in front of the audience and began José Alfredo Jiménez's elegy "Gracias." One of the Mexican people's most beloved idols was now the object of edgy satire, and the audience sang jovially along with Sabas as he ran through José Alfredo's most famous pieces. The satire and the mimicry definitely set Marichi Sol de América apart; I'd never seen another mariachi engage in anything remotely like this during performance.

All the other mariachi groups returned to the stage to play "La Negra" together, but the audience demanded more. Several songs later, they allowed the groups to take their bows.

The food was ready, the scent of grilled meat filling the night air. Mariachis lined up for tequila, beer, and Cokes. Stalls offered delicious tacos de cabeza (head meat tacos) and tacos de carne asada. After getting my tacos, I took a tall glass of dark beer and found a quiet place. I thought, "I must be dreaming." Tacos, cold Mexican beer, and a world-class mariachi concert, all on a moist night in a quiet little town.

About one in the morning, we got back on the bus.

Mariachi Sol de América got off the bus as we passed through Colima—they had another concert there the next day. Everyone else found a bench to stretch out on, and we headed for Guadalajara.

THE RISE OF MODERN MARIACHI

Modern mariachi began with the founding of Mariachi Vargas, the oldest and best-known mariachi group in the world. The year was 1898, and the place was the small village of Tecalitlán. Tecalitlán is a small farming village of the Bajio, the lowlands, tucked into the hills of western Jalisco.

MARIACHI VARGAS

Pepe Martínez Sr., Esteven Sandoval, and Andres Gonzalez on stage at Teatro Degollado, Guadalajara, Mexico. Photo © 2009 Jasper Schriber. BELOW: Mariachi Vargas. Private collection of Patricia Greathouse.

Mariachi Vargas played the music of their area, today called the Tecalitlán regional style. Founder Gaspar Vargas played guitarra de golpe, Manuel Mendoza played harp, and Lino Quintero and Refugio Hernández played violin. Little did they know at the time that they were laying the foundation of a dynasty that would come to define modern mariachi and last for more than a hundred years.

Mariachi Vargas's original members were part-time musicians, unable to read music, as were all traditional mariachis of their time. They often received goods in trade for their services.

In 1921, Gaspar's son Silvestre (1901–1985) joined Mariachi Vargas. By the early 1930s, the group was known regionally and had been playing at provincial festivals for many years.

Around 1931, during the days of Prohibition in the United States, Mariachi Vargas was contracted to play at a cantina in Tijuana. Just across the border from the United States, Tijuana had become a playground for thirsty Southern Californians. Up to that point, Vargas performed in their everyday clothes, but for this job, they began dressing in a style common to some peasants in parts of Jalisco—white pants and shirt of manta (coarse homespun cotton), a red woven belt,

red neckerchief, all topped with a straw hat. Mariachi historian Jonathan Clark stated that, according to Silvestre Vargas, although they would have liked to wear the traje de charro, manta was all they could afford.

THE SECOND GENERATION

In 1932, Silvestre Vargas took over as director of Mariachi Vargas. Under his leadership, the group added three new members over the next two years and gained a guitar and a guitarrón. Those instruments would become a permanent part of the modern mariachi ensemble.

Mariachi Vargas arrived in Mexico City in 1934 to perform for the presidential inauguration of Lázaro Elías Cárdenas. At that time, Concho Andrade's mariachi had been playing at Salon Tenampa in Plaza Garibaldi for years, and Cirilo Marmolejo's Mariachi Coculense played occasionally on the radio. José Marmolejo's Mariachi Tapatío was the most popular mariachi of the day and dominated the radio. Mariachi Vargas had a difficult time finding work.

In the 1930s, mariachi was still regional music from western Mexico. It had not yet attained the status of a national music, and more sophisticated orchestras were popular with many urban people. Life in the city was hard, and work was scarce for mariachis; however, Silvestre Vargas was able to secure a spot playing every two weeks on radio station XEB. Later, they graduated to XEW, then the most powerful radio station in Latin America; a regular slot on XEW's programming could establish the reputation of a group during the '30s and '40s.

President Cárdenas was a supporter of Mariachi Vargas. He not only brought them to Mexico City for his inauguration, he also helped them become an official band of the Mexico City Police Department. With that appointment, Mariachi Vargas moved permanently to Mexico City. Jonathan Clark reports Silvestre Vargas as saying that they wouldn't have made enough to live on in Mexico City without a regular paycheck from the police

department, and the department also bought them trajes de charro. In their official capacity, the group played in the homes of prominent citizens and politicians as well as in public parks.

There were several reasons why Mariachi Vargas eventually was able to supersede the other traditional mariachis of the day. First, Silvestre Vargas brought a new vision to his mariachi. He was interested in creating the very best group possible. Rather than playing at Plaza Garibaldi, Vargas focused on a relatively more elite clientele. He instilled a discipline that set Mariachi Vargas apart from the way other mariachis functioned. Insisting on sobriety, excellent musicianship, appropriate dress, and punctuality, he established a kind of military discipline. Also, according to historical accounts, Mariachi Vargas was a musically outstanding group from the start. Musicians talk about Gaspar Vargas's ability to play sones and the fine harp playing of Manuel Mendoza. The group won competitions in both Guadalajara and Mexico City.

Mariachi Vargas started in the movies in 1937 with a part in *Así Es Mi Tierra (That's the Way It Is in My Country)*, the first in a run of over 200 movies. During this time, Mariachi Vargas added "de Tecalitlán" to their name and signed a contract with RCA, making recordings alone and with well-known singers. Beginning in the 1940s, Mariachi Vargas also accompanied top solo artists on tour, in their recording sessions, and in live concerts.

Silvestre Vargas was a traditional small town mariachi. He was opposed to adding trumpet to his mariachi. He firmly felt that Mariachi Vargas should restrict itself to the type of regional music that mariachis had historically played. Although Silvestre told historian Jonathan Clark that he remembered a cornet playing briefly with his father's group in the 1910s, he himself resisted until public demand (and some say pressure from the owner of XEW) forced him to give the trumpet a try. In 1941, Miguel Martínez joined the group. Although it was a difficult fit at first, Martínez's supreme musicality and taste

Mariachi Vargas with dancers. Gaspar Vargas is on the far right, Silvestre Vargas is third from left, top row. Miguel Martínez is on the left. Private collection of Patricia Greathouse.

helped Mariachi Vargas de Tecalitlán rise to national prominence. He wasn't intrusive, and he didn't insert the trumpet in the bold way that many trumpet players of the day did.

Rubén Fuentes joined Mariachi Vargas as a violinist in 1944 and gradually changed the trajectory of the group. Fuentes was the musical director by 1950, and his work with them was largely responsible for defining and refining modern mariachi. He had a different background from the other men in the group. A classically trained violinist from a family of musicians, his musical taste was sophisticated, and wasn't tied to the traditional music of western Mexico.

During that period, some of the old guard left, alienated by the push to modernity that was required for mariachi to work efficiently in the contemporary world of recording and movies.

Fuentes retired from most performances in 1954 to become artistic director of RCA Victor. RCA branded Mariachi Vargas *El Mejor Mariachi del Mundo* (The Best Mariachi in the World). Fuentes also arranged music for most of the best singers of the day, including Jorge Negrete, Pedro Infante, Amalia Mendoza, Miguel Aceves Mejía, Antonio Águilar, Lola Beltrán, José Alfredo Jiménez, and Lucha Villa, and Mariachi Vargas accompanied them.

THE THIRD GENERATION

Although Miguel Martínez left the group for a short time in the early 1950s, by the time he returned, he had established the double-trumpet style now standard in modern mariachi.

Jesús Rodríguez de Híjar, who had been playing with Mariachi Perla de Occidente, became a violinist with Vargas in the mid-1950s. After Fuentes left, he became the music director. Rigoberto Alfaro, regarded as the finest mariachi guitarist of all time, joined the group in 1958, and they worked closely together on arrangements.

In 1967, Mariachi Vargas released "La Bikina" on an album called *La Nueva Dimensión (The New Dimension)*. "La Bikina" was full of chords, rhythms, and high violin positions that few mariachis of the day had the technique to master. With *La Nueva Dimensión*, Mariachi Vargas ushered mariachi into the second half of the twentieth century.

During this memorable period extremely talented and musically compatible men filled the ranks of the group. Rigoberto Alfaro, Jesús Rodríguez de Híjar, Heriberto Molino, and Miguel Martínez performed with others like them—Victor Cárdenas, Natividád Santiago, Mario Santiago, Federico Torres, Juan Pinzon, and Arturo Mendoza, among others—in a group that played mariachi music with passion, heart, and alegría.

Many of the men of that era were members for decades: Mario Santiago played with Vargas for almost fifty years.

Silvestre Vargas gradually retired from performing with Mariachi Vargas due to arthritis. As a man who had

Mariachi Vargas. Private collection of Patricia Greathouse.

started as a traditional village mariachi, he didn't have the violin technique to feel comfortable with the new music that Mariachi Vargas was performing. However, he continued to attend recording sessions and throw the *gritos* (shouts) heard in the recordings. He was always closely associated with the image of Mariachi Vargas.

Victor Cárdenas, who joined Mariachi Vargas as a vihuela player in 1970, was with the group long enough to have accompanied José Alfredo Jiménez. Born in Concepción de Buenos Aires, Jalisco, Cárdenas's brother and uncle were mariachis. He moved with his family to Mexico City when he was twelve years old, and before Silvestre Vargas invited him to join Mariachi Vargas, he played in various groups in restaurants. It had always been his greatest hope to join Vargas. As a member, he's been to Japan five times, and toured Hong Kong, Indonesia, Latin America, and the United States. In 2009, Cárdenas was still performing with the group, and Rubén Fuentes has asked him to stay with the group until he completes fifty years of playing.

THE FOURTH GENERATION

In 1975, Mariachi Vargas members sought out and recruited José "Pepe" Martínez Sr. (born in Tecalitlán, Jalisco, in 1941) to act as musical director of Mariachi Vargas. Pepe came from a family of musicians; his father was briefly a Mariachi Vargas harpist. He started playing a tiny vihuela when he was five and was playing professionally by the time he was eleven. He attended music school to become a note reader.

Pepe and his brother Fernando had founded Mariachi Nuevo Tecalitlán as young men in Jalisco, and had extensive experience with many mariachi groups. One of the Vargas members told me, "It's almost like being in the military, but if a musician doesn't like it, there are ten others waiting to take his place!"

Pepe Martínez is a shining example to the group. A high-energy, first-rate musician, he's a focused leader

Victor Cárdenas, a member of Mariachi Vargas for over forty years. Photo © 2009 Jasper Schriber.

onstage and a talented arranger. His celebrated composition "Violin Huapango" is a virtual concerto for mariachi.

Mariachi Vargas was invited to perform at the first mariachi conference in San Antonio in 1979. The next year, they were invited to teach as well. Within a couple of years, Vargas performed in concert with the San Antonio Symphony. It was a first for a mariachi group.

In 1988 and 1989, Mariachi Vargas accompanied Linda Ronstadt on her tour for *Canciones de Mi Padre*. It was an outstanding time for them, according to veteran mariachi Federico Torres; the tour lasted an unheard-of eleven months. It marked the breakthrough of mariachi into the mainstream American market. For the first time, Mariachi Vargas played to new audiences who hadn't grown up listening to mariachi music. Torres says of that time, "I tell you sincerely, and it's not a lie, that during the time we spent in the United States, we saw and did more than we had ever done in Mexico!"

Gustavo Alvarado Guillen, of Area de Rosales, Michoacán, and Federico Torres's compañero on trumpet, joined the group in 1990.

THE FIFTH GENERATION

Mariachi Vargas headlines each year at the Encuentro del Mariachi y la Charrería in Guadalajara. In addition to playing evening concerts for a week at the Teatro Degollado both solo and with an orchestra, they also travel to play at other venues during the celebrations, including the Campeonato Nacional Charro—the Mexican championship rodeo.

Vargas's ranks are full of a new generation of young, talented, and dynamic performers. They excel both in their technical ability and in their presentation.

José "Pepe" Martínez Jr. follows in his father's footsteps as violinist and vocalist. (His brothers are also mariachis; they play in Los Toritos, Mariachi Nuevo Tecalitlán, and Mariachi Sol de América.) Pepe Jr.'s been with Vargas since 1993. He took private music lessons when he was a boy and played with several other mariachis, including Mariachi de América, before joining Vargas.

Enrique Mendoza is the grandson of Silvestre Vargas and great-grandson of Gaspar. He plays the harp, as did his father, Arturo Mendoza, who played in Vargas for fifty years. Enrique's been with the group since 1999.

Esteven Sandoval is a dynamic front man and violinist from Tijuana. The most outstanding vocalist of the group, he's one of a new breed of electrifying mariachi performers whose dancing and singing charm audiences. He began violin when he was fifteen and has been with Vargas since 1999.

Esteven Sandoval, Lagos de Morenos, before International Charrería concert. Photo © 2009 Patricia Greathouse.

Daniel Martínez, Mariachi Vargas singer and violinist, Gustavo Alvarado Guíllen with trumpet. Photo © 2009 Jasper Schriber.

Arturo Vargas, Mariachi Vargas singer and guitarist. Photo © 2009 Jasper Schriber.

Arturo Vargas (no relation to Gaspar or Silvestre), a guitarist and singer famous for his falsetto, has been with Vargas since 2002. He was the featured singer with Mariachi de América on the PBS special *Mariachi: The Spirit of Mexico*. He gets enthusiastic applause when he approaches the microphone, smiling sweetly.

Alberto Alfaro is a violinist and silken-voiced soloist with silent-screen-star looks. Alfaro began studying music when he was twelve in Guadalajara and joined Mariachi Vargas in 1999. He was recruited from Mariachi Los Camperos.

Andres Gonzalez is one of the newest members. A fine singer and violinist from a mariachi family from Guadalajara, he also came from Mariachi de América.

Daniel Martínez (no relation to the other Martínezes) is living his life-long dream of playing with Vargas. Growing up as a poor boy with no education, he worked hard shining shoes and selling papers; he sang as he herded goats. He started as a guitarrón player and moved to Mexico City to try to make a career as a mariachi. He switched to violin; after playing on Plaza Garibaldi in numerous groups for seven years, he made it into Mariachi Sol de América.

Daniel Martínez joined Mariachi Vargas in 1985. He

Frederico Torres signs an autograph. Photo © 2009 Jasper Schriber.

Pepe Martínez Jr. at charrería. Photo © 2009 Jasper Schriber.

ABOVE: Alberto Alfaro. Photo © 2009 Jasper Scribner.
BELOW: Esteven Sandoval and Pepe Martínez, Sr. Photo ©
2009 Jasper Schriber.

Enrique Mendoza Vargas (left) and Enrique Santiago (right),
Mariachi Vargas. Photo © 2009 Jasper Schriber.

still works hard, taking bel canto lessons to keep his excellent voice in shape.

At over eighty years of age, Rubén Fuentes is the general director of Mariachi Vargas. When he's in the box during their performance at Teatro Degollado, everyone salutes him. He's the reason they're all there.

Mariachi Vargas continues to attend conferences in the United States and Mexico to the delight of new fans. Between conferences and performances, they now travel about half the year.

There is no other group as admired and imitated as Mariachi Vargas. They set the standard of style and taste, and their arrangements have become the standard repertoire. The old discipline, musicality, and meticulous attention to detail continue, and every hardworking mariachi in Mexico dreams of being invited to play with them.

THE RISE OF MARIACHI IN THE U.S.: MARIACHI COBRE

The first group of American-born musicians to form a hugely successful group, Mariachi Cobre led the new wave when the mariachi movement started in the United States. Having made their own path, they continue to follow a few guiding principles and the shared ideal of making Cobre the top group in the United States.

THE BEGINNING OF COBRE: LOS CHANGUITOS FEOS

Mariachi Cobre sprang from the inspiration of Father Charles Rourke, who started Los Changuitos Feos, the first youth mariachi in the United States, in Tucson in 1964. A first-year Irish-American priest from Schenectady, New York, Rourke was also a jazz pianist. He started the group as a Catholic Youth Organization project at All Saint's Parish in Tucson to keep boys off the streets and to reconnect them with their heritage.

Father Rourke had seen a group of young orphaned Mexican boys called Los Toritos perform in Guadalajara with a priest who had taught them to play and sing mariachi music. Rourke also listened to mariachi records with Father Arsenio Carrillo, the pastor of the cathedral, who was a Mexican music aficionado and owned a huge collection of old records. (Father Arsenio was also the uncle to future Mariachi Cobre members Randy and Stephen

CHANGUITO CARRILLO

Randy Carrillo, director of Mariachi Cobre, remembers joining Los Changuitos Feos in his early teens. He says:

It was British invasion time, and all I wanted to do was play rock and roll on my electric guitar. Meanwhile, there was lots of Mexican music going in the background in our house. My mom told me that Father Rourke had a group, and they were playing mariachi music. I wasn't enthusiastic, but she basically told me I was going to go, and she took me down to audition.

I heard the music, and thought "Wow!" I became very committed to learning mariachi music. I started on guitar, but I switched to guitarrón because it fascinated me; we'd take a break from rehearsal, and Father Rourke would put the guitarrón in the corner, and I'd go pick it up. I was very active in Los Changuitos Feos, as were my parents—we kept the group together in between sponsors. [A few years ago] my mom brought out the old calendar, and showed me my writing. I did the booking, and we rehearsed at our house.

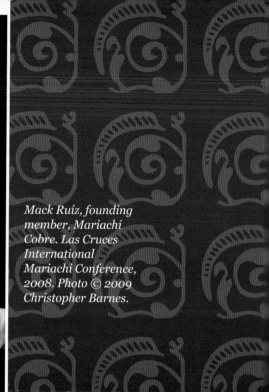

Mack Ruíz, founding member, Mariachi Cobre. Las Cruces International Mariachi Conference, 2008. Photo © 2009 Christopher Barnes.

Carrillo; they later arranged and recorded several pieces from Father Arsenio's collection that no other contemporary group had ever performed.)

Inspired by the orphans, the mariachi records, and his perceived need for young parishioners to develop pride in their Hispanic culture, Father Rourke decided to start a youth mariachi. Soon, a small group of boys was meeting in the basement of the All Saints Church and singing things like "Swing Low, Sweet Chariot." They soon grew into a group of ten guitar players and one trumpeter.

Gilbert Velez, one of the original boys in the group, says, "You couldn't find a Hispanic male to play violin to save your life. I was a guitar player already, so they found a beat-up old vihuela for me. They found a guitarrón, and someone played that. Father Rourke said we looked like a bunch of ugly monkeys, so he called us Los Changuitos Feos. We played all over, including Guadalajara, Chicago, and Washington, D.C. We finally earned enough money to buy uniforms, too! The violinists got their training in grade

school, and we built our own starter group with the older kids teaching the younger ones. In 1967, we auditioned for the *Ed Sullivan Show*."

When Father Rourke left, Father Butler replaced him, and Los Changuitos Feos continued to travel. They separated from the parish in the mid-1970s and parents took over management of the group.

In the 1980s, María Dolores Montañez became the first female in the group. Under her married name of Noperi, she went on to a professional mariachi career, becoming a member of Mariachi Reyna de Los Angeles. Today, Los Changuitos Feos has more young women than young men in the group. They celebrated their fortieth anniversary in 2004 with a reunion of former members from all over the country. Many had become professional musicians, but perhaps more importantly, hundreds of people have gotten a good education who might not have had the opportunity. Part of the Changuitos Feos philosophy from the beginning was to put education first, and each musician was guaranteed a college scholarship for his or her participation in the group.

BIRTH OF MARIACHI COBRE

When they graduated from Los Changuitos Feos in 1971, neither Mack Ruiz nor Randy Carrillo was ready to give up mariachi music. They knew Tucson would support a strong young group, and they knew they could recruit a large number of their fellow graduates. They invited Randy's younger brother, Stephen Carrillo, who was still in high school, to join them along with Gilbert Velez, one of the boys in Father Rourke's first group who had served in the military. Tony Saldivar, Paul Romo, and George Corrales also joined. Paul Romo's father, a local artist, came up with the name Mariachi Cobre, which means Copper Mariachi (at that time, Arizona was known as the Copper State).

Mariachi Cobre's first gig was a bar mitzvah, and they went on to become the house band at Los Yentes, a supper club in Tucson. They used to go to the Ronstadt family's house, where Linda would sing with them long before she began recording rancheras. She sang on their *Éste Es Mi Mariachi (This Is My Mariachi)* CD.

Cobre members had a long-time connection with the Disney corporation because they had performed at Disneyland for Cinco de Mayo when they were in Los Changuitos Feos. In early 1982, they made a demo tape and sent it to Sonny Anderson, talent booking agent for Disney, who remembered them. In 1973 and 1974, Cobre played summers at Disney World in Orlando. Randy met his future wife, Nancy, who also worked for Disney World.

EPCOT CENTER

In 1981, Disney was looking for a performing group for their Mexican Pavilion at EPCOT Center in Orlando. Cobre rented a room at the Tucson airport, and a group of executives flew out and auditioned them. At that time, Cobre was also right in the middle of preparations for the first Tucson mariachi conference. Nevertheless, they looked forward to leaving Tucson—they were young men eager for an adventure. When Disney offered them the job, they moved to Florida.

Mack Ruiz, violinist and cofounder of Cobre says, "We started our Disney dream then; we learned the Disney Magic. Those were great times! We had a lot of Mariachi Cobre parties. Then when we got older, we had family-oriented parties—kids breaking piñatas, and now some of us are grandparents watching grandkids breaking piñatas."

MARIACHI COBRE INTERNACIONAL

One of the most interesting things about Mariachi Cobre is the diversity of the group. The founding members were friends of about the same age who came from Los Changuitos Feos and the culture of Tucson, Arizona. Now mature family men, they play with young men from other parts of the United States and seasoned mariachis from Mexico. Mariachi Cobre has included women too. Randy Carrillo says:

> We've seen the numbers of women go from zero to huge in the time we've been in mariachi. There were no women in mariachi when we started! I respect them very much for their musicality. Vocally, it's a whole new dimension. And those women can play—two have been in Cobre, Rebecca Gonzales and Julie Davison. Julie was a Mexican woman with an Anglo name. She was a University of Arizona violin performance major.

The difference between training and attitude surrounding mariachi culture in Mexico and the United States is easily reflected in the personal histories of Mariachi Cobre members. The men from Tucson have seen firsthand how their perspective and life experience differ from that of their Mexican colleagues. The young men in Los Changuitos Feos didn't play in cantinas; formal education came first and mariachi was an exciting extracurricular activity.

For the Mexicans, who learned mariachi at their fathers' knees, playing mariachi music was vocational training. It was work, and they contributed to the welfare and upkeep of their families.

There are currently four Cobre members from Mexico, all violinists: brothers Hector and Carlos Gama, Antonio Hernández, and Arturo Pasalagua. The Gamas' father, Pablo Gama Chavez of Mariachi Gama, arranged pieces for many well-known Mexican singers. He worked hard to support his family and to ensure that all nine of his children, seven boys and two girls, learned to play violin. The continuation of mariachi music within his family was important to him, and all the boys became mariacheros.

Carlos and Hector took private lessons with Maestro Robert Vaska. A classical violinist, he was famous for his association with symphony conductors and learned musicians. Hector quotes him as saying, "I'm not going to teach you mariachi! Take my technique and apply it to your music!" Vaska also taught several Mariachi Vargas de Tecalitlán violinists and Cobre's Antonio Hernández, starting a minor revolution in Mexico. Until his work with mariachi violinists, there were few who had the opportunity to study with teachers of his caliber and to learn advanced violin technique.

The Gamas started taking violin lessons when they were quite young. At the ages of twelve and thirteen, their father helped them became members of a group sponsored by the Mexican government called Mariachi Monumental, an organization of 200 musicians.

Life was hard when the Gamas were young. They had to study academics and to work as mariachis at the same time. They attended José F. Vazquez's Escuela Libre de Música y Declamación (The Free School of Music and Recitation), and there they learned solfège, theory, and notation. There wasn't a school for mariachi music in Mexico; the Gamas learned from other mariachis and from playing in Santos

Miguel Molina and Stephen Carrillo, Mariachi Cobre trumpet section, Las Cruces International Mariachi Conference, 2008. Photo © 2009 Christopher Barnes.

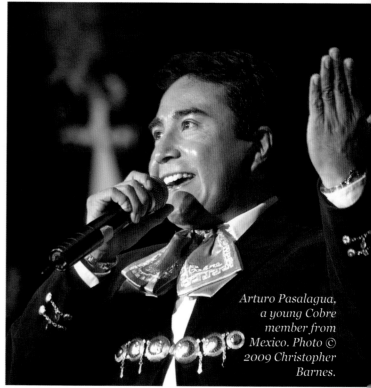

Arturo Pasalagua, a young Cobre member from Mexico. Photo © 2009 Christopher Barnes.

Israel Molina, front. Back, left to right: Mario Trujillo, Carlos Gama, and Antonio Hernández. Las Cruces, 2007. Photo © 2009 Christopher Barnes.

Marmolejo's group. Santos was a descendent of Cirilo Marmolejo, and Pablo Gama also performed with his sons in the group.

As adults, Carlos and Hector worked with all the big-name groups in Mexico City, either as group members or in the recording studio, including Mariachi Vargas de Tecalitlán, Mariachi 70 de Pepe López, Mariachi México de Pepe Villa, and two Gama family groups called Mariachi Gamamil and Mariachi 2000. The brothers always worked side by side and they always got along.

It was a big step when Hector decided to move permanently to the United States. He hated to leave Carlos. "We were always together, we started out riding the bus to our violin lessons together, we always played together in the same groups, and to this day we never fight. . . ."

"I was so sad to have lost my brother, and then I found another set of brothers in Cobre," Hector says. "But now I have my brother Carlos here with me, too, and it's wonderful!"

Randy Carrillo, director of Mariachi Cobre, does all the business arrangements and logistics for the group. Photo © 2009 Christopher Barnes.

They lost another brother, Raul, who died as a martyr to the hard life of a mariachi. Mariachi Gamamil was contracted to perform for the president of Mexico. Plácido Domingo was the featured performer, and he and the president had planned on singing a duet. A storm came up, and the orchestra that was accompanying Domingo left the stage; however, the mariachis had to stand out in the cold rain and wind to perform. Domingo and the president sang their duet, and the mariachis got soaked. "Our brother Raul had a very weak heart, and three days later he was dead of cardiac arrest," Carlos says sadly.

Hector is bullish on Cobre: "It's the best group I've ever been in; they're so positive—and mariachi is full of bad politics! This group has no problem with drugs, alcohol, or poor attitudes. During our breaks, the guys go running, read books, study the music, or practice. In my previous groups, the members would play cards or drink." Hector is known to practice pieces like the "Bruch Violin Concerto" on his breaks during conferences.

Antonio Hernández, the son of a mariachi and a native of Guadalajara, is largely self-educated. His natural curiosity prompts him to read between shows at EPCOT Center.

When Hernández was fourteen, he heard the "Brahms Violin Concerto" on the classical music station, and he asked his father if he could learn to play violin. His first real violin teacher was Ignacio Camarena, who was head of strings at the University of Guadalajara.

When Hernández was about sixteen, he moved to Mexico City, where he played with Mariachi Juvenil Imperial. There he studied classical violin with Maestro Vaska, also the Gamas' teacher. He played at Plaza Garibaldi during that period, and met Carlos and Hector Gama when they all played in Mariachi 70. Legendary former Mariachi Vargas trumpeter Miguel Martínez played in the group as well.

Hernández began to tour with performers who came to the United States. He says:

In 1976, I traveled to the USA with a mariachi band accompanying a couple of Mexican singers, and let me tell you, they were just pop singers dressed in charro suits. They didn't represent anything cultural or authentically Mexican. I was subjected to a lot of bad music during that time.

Disillusioned with the lack of disciplined musicality and training in the groups he was playing with, Hernández quit mariachi. After several years of playing in symphonies and freelancing in the United States, he moved to Tampa, Florida, in 1983. Hernández was playing evenings in the Colombia Restaurant, when Cobre members met him. He says the only reason he returned to mariachi is because he heard in Mariachi Cobre the real discipline and musicality he was seeking, and the music they were playing was real. To him, they were the best. Randy called him on Christmas Eve 1989, and said, "Can you come to rehearsal?" On January 28, 1990, Disney hired him. He still freelances with symphonies whenever possible, and after the Las Cruces conference, Hernández stayed to play the Shostakovich Fifth Symphony with the El Paso Symphony.

Hernández feels strongly about mariachi education in the United States, and he does his best to share what he knows through conferences. He says:

> I went through a lack of training when I played mariachi in Mexico, and I legitimized it under the guise of style. It only increased my deficiencies.
>
> Mariachi teaching should be secondary to violin teaching. Classical training is the foundation of violin playing, and mariachi players and teachers are in great need of it. First I learned to play mariachi, then I had to go back to my teacher and learn how to play violin. Violinists need foundations in classical training, and there is no substitute for that. If you're trying to convince me that bad playing habits are a style, I will disagree. The word *sobón* [the slides heard in the violins] shouldn't be applied to music on any planet—there's a word for it—*glissando,* and we should use the proper term. Sobón is slang, street talk, for something that is a legitimate musical technique.
>
> People like Hector and I are running away from Garibaldi, and here in the United States,

Hector Gama, Las Cruces, New Mexico. Photo © 2009 Christopher Barnes.

they're running toward it, thinking that kind of playing is the true mariachi sound. We should use good technique.

MARIACHI COBRE'S TRADITION AND CULTURE

Mariachi Cobre's nucleus of Mack Ruiz and Randy and Stephen Carrillo have been together for very long time—thirty-six years. Others with many years of service are Robert Martínez (thirty), Israel Molina (twenty-six years), and Miguel Molina (seventeen). Frank Grijalva was with Cobre for thirty-three years—he was their arranger for both mariachi and orchestra music. He had formal music training and was very good at it.

"Something about Cobre appeals to many musicians, and they wind up staying a long time, unlike many groups, where the turnover is rapid," says Randy. The old guard has forty years of shared anecdotes; there is a lot of chemistry between them, which comes off on stage. Between 2005 and 2007, they lost three members—Chris Figueroa, Mario Trujillo (who has since returned to the group), and Frank Grijalva all went to the Clark County School District, Las Vegas, Nevada. They had played together for sixteen years, and it was hard. Ruiz says:

We have a kind of extra-sensory perception. We can just look at each other and know what's going on. It takes a new member two to three years until they understand that we don't always have to speak to communicate. Becoming a culturally diverse, international group was a change for us, and we make it a point that anybody who comes into the group is accepted. I like the feeling of playing with a group that's very musical. This group is loaded with great singers and great musicians.

ABOVE: Antonio Hernández, Las Cruces, New Mexico, 2007. Photo © 2009 Christopher Barnes. BELOW: Carlos Gama, Las Cruces, New Mexico, 2007. Photo © 2009 Christopher Barnes.

Cobre's position is enviable in the mariachi world; work hours at EPCOT Center allow them time to be with their families. They travel five to seven times a year for conferences or special appearances with orchestras or at festivals. As employees of a corporation, they have benefits—something unheard of in the mariachi world.

The culture of Mariachi Cobre is different from that of most other groups. Randy says:

> I try to do this group as democratically as possible, and try to be inclusive of as many opinions as possible. With musicians, especially, the egos and the opinions are endless. We don't agree on everything. Age differences can create huge conflicts, and there's a little bit of that in our group, but it's not bad. I don't want to lose credibility and trust by being a tyrant. I work with childhood friends, and now and then being the boss is hard. We talk, and we decide things together. Everybody works toward common goals, and all the guys in our group have a good work ethic. We try to come to an understanding. There are some groups that have very authoritarian leadership, and I understand why that is, because keeping a group together is very difficult.

Cobre has performed with thirty-six orchestras. They consider their tour with the Boston Pops to be one of the best things they have ever done. Randy says, "The highlight of that tour was being able to collaborate with people of the caliber of Keith Lockhart and the musicians in the orchestra. The pleasure of being able to work with someone as musically and mentally capable as he is was fabulous. Cobre's emphasis has always been on the high level of ensemble, and it added another dimension. It was a great experience."

COBRE'S MUSICAL INNOVATION

Randy sums up his view of what Mariachi Cobre has contributed to the modern developments in the genre:

People say mariachi music has changed—they play cumbias, they play big band. I don't think that's deep change; it's just playing another music mariachi style. Playing other genres isn't a deep change in the fiber of the music—what we have done, the change in harmonies, has evolved the music. We're known for our vocal ability; Stephen is the musical director of Mariachi Cobre, and he writes out all the vocal parts, which is unusual. If you're going to sing a solo, take some liberty. If you're singing together, sing together. Stephen's way of voicing harmonies has evolved mariachi music in an elemental way. We also play pieces that nobody else plays, like "La Rafaelita," which was recorded by Juan and Amalia Mendoza as "Duetto Tariacuri."

Cobre pays close attention to their staging, breaking up the voices so that they get a good vocal blend. The group has worked with vocal coach Manny Lujan for twenty years to improve their vocal technique and learn bel canto–style singing. Teaching good vocal health and technique is an important part of what they do at conferences. The group vocalizes each day before performances, and trumpet player Miguel Molina vocalizes all day long, according to his colleagues. Ruiz tells the story of Molina practicing air trumpet while driving on the freeway, hand held high and lips buzzing.

Stephen Carrillo's voicing is unique in the violin, trumpet, and vocal parts. It departs from the typical parallel thirds and three-part harmonies standard in mariachi arrangements. Sometimes he writes chords in open sixths, which means that there is an edginess to harmony that sounds elemental and raw, although it's both refined and sophisticated. He likes to hold a note or two in the harmony and move the top part. Stephen says, "The main difference in what I do is that the chording has less movement. It makes the ensemble fuller when harmony parts

*Las Coronelas, 1954.
Private collection of
Patricia Greathouse.*

don't move in parallel structure." Sometimes he keeps it simple, but it's always interesting, hard to learn, and unpredictable. Mariachi Cobre's dedication to excellence and education is admirable.

WOMEN IN MARIACHI

Women have been hog-tied by strictures—rules, roles, and family—since Eve first bit into the apple. Once women got the chance to play mariachi, they had to do it in long straight skirts, high-heeled boots, heavy-duty makeup, big earrings, and styled hair. Of course they were beautiful and exotic looking, but they often got the message that they would never play as well as the men. Nevertheless, smart, motivated women have joined the highest ranks of mariachi, adding a colorful and dynamic dimension to what was once an exclusive club. Today, they are giving the men a run for their money, winning competitions at conferences and showing that they can have it all—family, career, and music.

MEXICAN WOMEN PIONEERS IN MARIACHI

Jesús Jaúregui, eminent scholar of traditional mariachi, writes about a *mariachera* (female mariachi) named Doña Rosa Quirino (1891–1969) who lived in the Nayarit altiplano many years ago. When challenged, she was tough enough to whip grown men. She carried a pistola, was said to have used it, and once felled a town bully with her knife. Strong and independent, she organized her own mariachi group and liked to live her life as freely as a man. Doña Rosa not only played wherever she pleased, as head of her own group she defied anyone to stop her.

Few Mexican women of her time lived the life of Doña Rosa, however. Social mores dictated the role of women and kept them in their place until very recently, and that place was in the house, cooking and caring for children, not playing mariachi music.

Until the dawning of the women's liberation movement, few Mexican women had the force of will to challenge society openly. Those who wanted to be mariacheras were not allowed to play in men's groups and had to form their own.

Carlota Noriega formed Mariachi Las Coronelas in Mexico City in the 1940s. They toured within Mexico, as well as outside the country. In the 1950s, Adelita Chavez formed Las Adelitas, naming the group after herself as well as the iconic women heroes of the Mexican Revolution. Estrellas de México was a prominent female group in the '60s, and the famous Mariachi Femenil Xochitl followed in the '80s and is now over twenty years old. Alma Rocío Corona started Mariachi Las Perlitas Tapatías in Guadalajara in 1989, which bills itself as the first all-female mariachi, although it clearly is not.

Lucha Reyes's portrait in Salon Tenampa, Plaza Garibaldi, Mexico City. Photo © 2009 Jasper Schriber.

THE CANCIÓN RANCHERA DIVAS

Canción ranchera divas, the equivalent of Patti Page, Julie London, and Edie Gorme in the United States, enchanted the public because they left behind the Mexican ideal of woman as Madonna to personify lovers, sufferers, and sinners. Lucha Reyes, née María de la Luz Flores Aceves (1906–1944), was the first woman to record Mexican music backed by mariachis; her recordings are legendary for their passion and heart-rending emotion. Born into poverty in Guadalajara, she had a very difficult early life. After moving to Mexico City with her mother, she sang corridos of the Revolution in a tent on a public plaza to survive.

As a young woman, Reyes toured a great deal; she spent several years singing in Los Angeles, where she studied to be a lyric soprano and was successful in the Mexican-American community. On a tour of Germany, she developed a terrible case of laryngitis and lost her voice for a year. When she recovered, her voice was coarse and raw

Maria Teresa Ortega
Martínez of Mariachi
Femenil Nuevo
Tecalitlán, Tecomán,
Colima, 2007. Photo
© 2009 Patricia
Greathouse.

sounding. She was no longer a soprano, and the mariachi trademark *estilo bravía* (savage or wild style) was born. With the help of Silvestre Vargas (leader of Mariachi Vargas de Tecalitlán), she began to sing rancheras on XEW, the Voice of Latin America.

Reyes recorded many songs that have become the basis for the modern female mariachi repertoire. She became known as "La Tequilera" after recording one of her most popular hits of the same name. Unfortunately, her life ended early. Her beloved husband left her for another woman, and she died on June 25, 1944, of an overdose of drugs and alcohol.

Reyes's legacy is immense: as the first woman to enter the arena of popular Mexican recording stars, she opened the door and defined the style for her younger "sisters," Lola Beltrán, Amalia Mendoza, and Lucha Villa. They interpreted traditional men's rancheras like "El Rey" with gusto and strength, achieving huge popularity, financial success, and relative autonomy. Like their male counterparts, they were not mariachis—by definition mariachis belong to groups and play instruments. However, the ranchera divas are important to mariachi tradition, particularly for the stylistic example they set for female mariachis.

MARIACHI FEMENIL NUEVO TECALITLÁN

The female branch of one of Mexico's mariachi dynasties, Mariachi Femenil Nuevo Tecalitlán contains family members of Mariachi Nuevo Tecalitlán founders Pepe Martínez (current director of Mariachi Vargas de Tecalitlán) and Fernando Martínez. The young women in this group wanted to take up the tradition of mariachi, and the group members see each other as sisters. They know that in order to make a successful group, they all have to pull together.

In Japan they cage a young nightingale with an older bird that sings beautifully so that it will learn skill by imitation. So it is with musicians. The women of Mariachi Femenil Nuevo Tecalitlán are continuing the family tradition of excellence and showmanship after a lifetime of good examples.

FEMALE MARIACHIS IN THE UNITED STATES

In the Mexican mariachi tradition, boys followed their fathers in a musical apprenticeship; formal education in mariachi did not exist. Education in the United States was not only formalized in a class setting, it was open to both sexes of any ethnicity. When the mariachi education movement started in the United States in the early '60s, women joined classes. It was the beginning of a radical change in how people became mariachi musicians.

Initially, women filled the violin sections, having come from public school classes where they had been classically trained—violin was a "girl's instrument." Consequently, finding women to play the other instruments in the mariachi ensemble, particularly the guitarrón and trumpet, "boys' instruments," was nearly impossible. Public school mariachi classes have provided a way for both genders to learn the basics of mariachi music on whatever instrument they chose.

LINDA RONSTADT'S MARIACHI CONNECTION

Linda Ronstadt, who credits Lola Beltrán as a role model, was helpful in bringing mariachi music into the United States at a time when it was known mostly by Mexican-Americans in the border regions. Ronstadt is not a mariachi, nor has she dedicated her life to singing canción ranchera. She is a talented singer with wide musical interests, who, after singing a few pieces with Mariachi Vargas in Tucson, was inspired to make an album of Mexican music.

Ronstadt was very familiar with the genre, for she grew up listening to her father Gilbert's vintage Mexican

The cover for Linda Ronstadt's Canciones de Mi Padre *took its inspiration from this painting by Jesús Helguera. Courtesy of Calendarios Landin.*

recordings. An avid music aficionado and singer, he often had the young Mariachi Cobre over to his ranch to make music.

When Ronstadt decided to record her first Spanish-language CD, the aptly named *Canciones de Mi Padre (Songs of My Father)*, she remembered those classic recordings and asked Rubén Fuentes, the arranger and owner of Mariachi Vargas de Tecalitlán, and Peter Asher, formerly of Peter and Gordon, the English pop duo, to produce it.

Her recordings helped to inspire the mariachi music renaissance in the United States. *Canciones de Mi Padre* and a second, *Mas Canciones* (More Songs), were both huge sellers and won Grammy Awards for Best Mexican-American Performance. As an established pop star, she brought a huge number of new fans to mariachi music and lit a new fire for old fans.

THE FIRST ALL-FEMALE GROUPS

A small handful of women pioneers were determined to start their own groups in the United States. In 1976, María

Elena Muñoz, a well-known ranchera singer in the Los Angeles area, began Mariachi Las Generalas, the first all-female group in the United States. Made up of the wives and mothers of professional mariachis, the group met strong resistance. Husbands didn't like the idea of their wives entertaining in cantinas, even though most of the women wanted to play the mariachi mass or to accompany community events. Some of the husbands went so far as to break their wives' instruments to stop them from playing.

A horrible tragedy ended the pioneering efforts of a second all-women's group, Mariachi Estrella, of Topeka, Kansas. Teresa Cuevas organized the group in 1977 to play the mariachi mass for her parish church. In 1981, they decided to branch out and perform in the community. At one of their first professional jobs, the skywalk at the Hyatt Hotel in Topeka collapsed and four of the six band members were killed along with 110 other people. Mariachi Estrella continued afterward as a mixed-gender group, and cofounder Teresa Cuevas, now in her eighties, still performs with them. An eighteen-foot monument to the women now stands on the grounds of the Topeka Performing Arts Center.

REBECCA GONZALES UNLOCKS THE DOOR

The first woman to break into professional mariachi in the United States, Rebecca Gonzales was born and raised in San Jose, California. Growing up, she played classical violin in the public school orchestra program. In 1972, during a rehearsal in Fresno with the California All-State Honors Orchestra, Gonzales met Mark Fogelquist of Mariachi Uclatlán who was recruiting students for his class at San Jose City College. When he told her he was teaching a class in mariachi music, Gonzales asked, "What's mariachi?"

After Gonzales took Fogelquist's class, she began performing with Mariachi Los Abajeños de Isidro Rivera. One of her colleagues in the group urged her to get vocal coaching, pointing out that if she was serious about being a professional mariachi, she would have to sing. A year later, Fogelquist came to hear the group, and after hearing Gonzales sing, he asked her to join Mariachi Uclatlán. She moved to Los Angeles in 1974 to become the first woman ever to join the group. After she had performed a year with Mariachi Uclatlán, Nati Cano invited her to join the previously all-male Mariachi Los Camperos. Gonzales says, "Women had played with their husbands in groups before, but none had been able to join a group of the caliber of Los Camperos on their own merit. As the first woman to infiltrate a famous all-male show group, I felt honored to be mentored by top-notch mariachi musicians. They were very courteous and gentlemanly toward me. Initially, I felt all eyes were on me, but soon things relaxed."

It was an exciting time for Gonzales and for fans of mariachi. Television, newspaper, and magazine reporters interviewed her because of her ground-breaking entry into (in Gonzales's words) "the new and

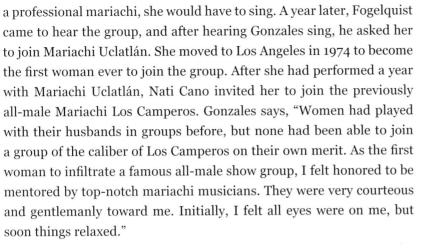

RIGHT: Rebecca Gonzales and BELOW: with Los Camperos.
Photos courtesy of Rebecca Gonzales.

Los Camperos

Rebecca Gonzales sings at the Hollywood Bowl with Mariachi Los Gavilanes in 1996. She belonged to the group from 1995 to 1999. Photo courtesy of Rebecca Gonzales.

improved Mariachi Los Camperos." Gonzales had become a role model for young women in mariachi. She says, "They thought, if Rebecca can do it, so can we!"

In 1983, Gonzales joined Mariachi Cobre and performed at Disney World's EPCOT Center for a year, an experience she loved. In 2004, Rebecca Gonzales was inducted into the Tucson Music Festival Hall of Fame. She still feels that the ideal group sound is a mixture of male and female voices. The balance of highs and lows offers a wider range of musical nuance and therefore, more variety.

Gonzales currently teaches violin using the Suzuki Method at a music store in Palos Verdes, California, and works as a freelance mariachi performer.

LAURA SOBRINO: MARIACHI PERFORMER AND EDUCATOR

Laura Sobrino, the musical director of Mariachi Mujer 2000, grew up in Watsonville, California. She learned violin in the public schools and played in a youth symphony, but it was through the inspiration of a college teacher, UCLA ethnomusicologist David Kilpatrick Martin, that she began to play mariachi music.

Sobrino specialized in Mexican folk music under an independent study major in college. When she first heard mariachi music in class, she knew that she could play it too, and she became a member of University of California Santa Cruz's Mariachi Santa Cruz in 1975.

In 1978, Sobrino moved to Los Angeles to perform in Mark Fogelquist's Mariachi Uclatlán, where she learned a vast amount of mariachi repertoire. A few years later, Mariachi Los Galleros's director Pedro Rey Hernández gave her a six-month performing audition. She became their first female member and eventually became one of the violin section leaders.

When Pedro Rey's brother José Hernández formed his own group, Mariachi Sol de Mexico, in 1986, he invited Sobrino to join, and they started performing shows in Hernández's Cielito Lindo restaurant.

Sobrino performed with Sol de Mexico except during her pregnancies. At a little over six feet tall, she was hard to miss, and there were still some old-fashioned people who felt it was inappropriate for a pregnant woman to be playing mariachi music. However, she did continue to play with other groups, looking even more womanly in a beautiful Yucatecan flowered dress.

In 1993, Hernández asked Sobrino to be in charge of a new women's group he was forming, called Mariachi Reyna de Los Angeles. She was the music director of Reyna for two years. After Mariachi Reyna, Sobrino became a charter member of Mariachi Mujer 2000, founded in 1999; she continues today as the music director.

The Tucson International Mariachi Hall of Fame honored Sobrino in April 2004. Using her training as an ethnomusicologist, Sobrino began documenting the history of women performers in mariachi in the '90s. In 2008, she launched a Web site of her research, The Female Pioneers in Mariachi Music, www.mujeresenelmariachi. com, which includes the history of early Mexican and U.S. female mariachis. A registry for female mariachis groups is also on the site. In addition to her performances, Sobrino teaches school groups, private lessons, and conference classes. She directs mariachi ensembles at University of California Riverside, Chaffey College, East Los Angeles College, and Rio Hondo College. Although she is so important in the world of mariachi, her first job is "to be her two children's mother." She and her husband Dan Sobrino run the Mariachi Publishing Company, a music transcription business she started in 1995.

MARIACHI REYNA DE LOS ANGELES

Formed in 1994 as the first women's show mariachi in the United States, Mariachi Reyna de Los Angeles still performs regularly at José Hernández's Cielito Lindo restaurant in El Monte, California. After playing a concert with Mariachi las Perlitas from Guadalajara, Hernández decided to create a professional all-female mariachi that would compete with the best men's groups. He recruited Laura Sobrino to be their first director, knowing she had the leadership qualities and experience necessary to help younger members.

A documentary released in 2007, *Compañeras (Comrades)* details the lives, joys, and struggles of the women of Mariachi Reyna.

Many professional women mariachis, among them Cindy Reifler, Marisa Orduño, and Laura Sobrino have benefited from working under outstanding musician and arranger José Hernández in Mariachi Reyna.

CINDY SHEA AND MARIACHI DIVAS

A blond, blue-eyed trumpet-playing woman strikes some people as a fish out of water. That doesn't bother Cindy Shea, the founder and director of Mariachi Divas. She says "I've gotten to the point where I feel if you like what I do, good. If you don't, there are a hundred other people who do. I don't defend myself anymore!"

Shea started playing the trumpet in public school when she was eight years old. It was the beginning of her unconventional musical life. After graduation, she studied classical and jazz trumpet at the University of California at Fullerton and planned to be a teacher.

Patricia Martin of Mariachi Reyna. San Jose Feria, 2007. Photo © 2009 Patricia Greathouse.

Judith Kamel of Mariachi Reyna, Las Cruces, New Mexico, 2008. Photo © 2009 Christopher Barnes.

Cindy Shea (right) and
Esperanza Hernández
of Mariachi Divas.
Photo courtesy of
Cindy Shea.

Arturo Sandoval, who Shea calls the best living trumpeter in the world, heard her play and invited her to come to Florida International University to be his student. He gave her a full jazz performance scholarship, and she dropped everything to study with Sandoval for three years.

After moving back to Los Angeles, Shea started playing Latino and salsa music, performing with Celia Cruz as part of her West Coast salsa band.

An all-female mariachi, Las Alondras, heard her play and asked her to join them. She had never played mariachi before, but she played with them for six months. Although she loved mariachi, the strict arrangements didn't leave room for improvisation, and she really missed tropical music and playing a jazz solo from time to time. She came up with the idea of melding jazz and tropical rhythms—salsa, cumbia, merengue, cha cha cha, and mariachi music—and founded Mariachi Divas in November 1999.

The diverse cultures of the many women who have been Divas over the years have left their imprint on the group. It's reflected in the instruments they use as well as in their arrangements. In a full stage show, Divas play congas, bongos, cajón, percussion, flutes, maracas, and both the güiro and the güira in addition to traditional mariachi instruments.

In the beginning, people criticized Shea for what she was doing—it was different, and "it wasn't mariachi." Shea calls one style she created with the Divas ranchengue—a cross between ranchera and merengue. "The beauty of Divas is that we don't have to use all the instruments at every performance—we use them when we do a big stage show, but we can go smaller or bigger and keep the same style, the same fun. Music evolves. Rock-and-roll, classical music, jazz; everything changes. I love Elvis, but what if we were stuck with him forever? I didn't choose our style just to be different; everything evolved naturally." Mariachi Divas CD Canciones de Amor was nominated for Best Regional Mexican Album in 2008.

MARISA ORDUÑO AND MARIACHI MUJER 2000

Marisa Orduño was the first guitarrón player of Mariachi Reyna, playing with them for seven years. After she graduated from college she planned on being a teacher; however, she found herself missing the show aspects of performance and what she calls the comadreship of the other women.

In 1999, Orduño hand-picked women from all over the country who were classically trained or had innate talent and wanted to work hard, and she founded Mariachi Mujer 2000. Orduño's dream was to have a technically challenging repertoire that would be equal to the top men's show groups.

Mariachi Mujer 2000 has played in the Hollywood Bowl, and for Oprah Winfrey, Barack Obama, and for Maria Shriver and Arnold Schwarzenegger's tribute to women artists and role models at the California Arts Museum, where their CD and their trajes were exhibited.

Mariachi Mujer 2000 continues to draw members from all over. Women commute from San Jose, Whittier, and other California communities, as well as El Paso, Texas, to play with Mariachi Mujer 2000. They spend a long weekend once a year putting their show together with Laura Sobrino, the music director. Sometimes they send music ahead for the women to learn, but not always. Orduño points out that the women are such seasoned professionals that they can handle the pressure and intensity. They usually have a refresher rehearsal the night before or the day of a concert for their eight big performances each year.

Mariachi Mujer 2000 is currently the only female show group totally owned and directed by women. Education is very important to them. All of the women in Mariachi Mujer 2000 either hold bachelor's degrees, multiple credentials, or are attending a college or university. They continue to travel the United States to teach and perform at mariachi conferences in Tucson, Denver, Kansas City, and Fresno. They performed at the 2008 Summer Olympics in Beijing, China.

Mariachi Mujer 2000: Vanessa Parada, Suemy Gonzalez, Crystal Cañez, Laura Sobrino, Marisa Orduño, Carla Díaz, Patricia Fernández, Amelia Garcia, Jazmin Morales, Mima Santiago. Photo courtesy of Marisa Orduño.

Monica Montoya of Mariachi Tenampa. Photo © 2009 Christopher Barnes.

MONICA MONTOYA OF MARIACHI TENAMPA

No one thought New Mexico's premier mariachi, all-male Mariachi Tenampa, would ever hire a woman. Monica Montoya had worked on recordings with them and played in shows when they needed a substitute, so she was pleasantly shocked when she was asked to be an official member of the group.

Tenampa had resisted adding a woman for many years, although there were several good players who had worked hard to get into the group. Al Gurule, the director, says that they had been accused of being male chauvinists many times. Montoya tells of stepping forward to play the difficult violin solo in *"El Gustito,"* while a young man in the front row watched her intently. Afterward he approached and told her that she "played real good for a girl."

Tamarah Lucero has since joined Mariachi Tenampa, and Montoya is thrilled to have the company.

AMELIA GARCIA OF MARIACHI TAPATÍO AND MARIACHI MUJER 2000

Amelia Garcia is the director, soloist, and trumpet player of Mariachi Tapatío as well as a member of Mariachi Mujer 2000. She's a good example of the motivated, hard-working, and talented women trying to make it in the world of mariachi today. Dubbed "little trumpet sister" by some of her male peers, she has grown her group into a sophisticated and technically excellent mariachi. She has encountered little resistance to her participation in mariachi and a great deal of support.

Women who have succeeded in the male world of mariachi have had to be tougher, more determined, and to some extent more talented. They have also tended to be intensely invested in education—both their own and that of their students. Many of the pioneering women who made it into the previously male-only club of mariachi music were faced with the same challenges as women entering business, academia, or the visual arts. The history of women's success in mariachi runs parallel to their progress toward equality in other areas, and they led the way for their younger followers. To see what they've accomplished is a true inspiration.

Mariachi Feminil Flor Huasteca, a professional group whose members come from the University of Texas-Pan American. Photos © 2009 Christopher Barnes.

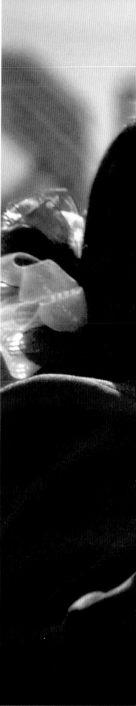

Maritza Loya (left) and Amelia Garcia (right) with Mariachi Tapatío, Student Showcase, Mariachi Spectacular, Albuquerque, New Mexico, 2007. Photo © 2009 Christopher Barnes.

EDUCATION AND CONFERENCES

A passion for mariachi music has spread around the world by radio, recordings, and television. It claims professional and amateur musicians and fans from Latin America to Europe, Scandinavia, and the Balkans. A Japanese mariachera sings along with Mariachi Vargas occasionally. However, there is no place where mariachi education has reached the same level of popularity as it has in the United States. Although the centers of the mariachi movement in the United States are Tucson, San Antonio, and Los Angeles, school groups have flourished from places as far removed as Wenachee, Washington, and New York's Harlem.

THE BEGINNING OF MARIACHI EDUCATION

The mariachi education movement began in the early 1960s in the United States, surprisingly, and not in Mexico. Although mariachi is a completely Mexican genre, formal mariachi education is still in its infancy there.

In the 1960s, groups like the Weavers, The Limelighters, The Kingston Trio, and Peter, Paul, and Mary embraced folk music from all over the globe. They toured college campuses, inspiring students to pick up a guitar and sing. Like the times, the ideas were "a' changin'," and the hands-on study of traditional music became accredited in colleges across the United States. Prior to this time, the only people who played folk music were carriers of the culture, but in the '60s and '70s, people not only got into folk music, they began to learn folk dancing and to dress in native costumes, too.

In 1961, at the University of California, Los Angeles, a few ethnomusicology students participated in the first mariachi class ever given. The Institute of Ethnomusicology at UCLA soon added a performance program. A graduate student in ethnomusicology in 1961–62, Donn Borchardt founded Mariachi Uclatlán (literally UCLA land) as part of his graduate studies. Tragically, Borchardt died during a field trip to Guadalajara in 1965.

Early on, Mariachi Uclatlán learned its music from recordings, but they soon hired Jesús "Don Chuy" Sánchez as "ethnic adviser." A veteran mariachi from Jalisco, Sánchez took over teaching, and he encouraged women to join the group, which marked the beginning of women in mixed-group mariachis.

Graduate student Mark Fogelquist, an accomplished violinist, joined the group in 1966. He had fallen in love with mariachi music during a summer in Guadalajara and had majored in music as an undergraduate. Fogelquist wrote his master's thesis on the son jalisciense, and spent a great deal of time with Tijuana mariachis. Along with fellow UCLA ethnomusicologist Dan Sheehy, they became the eminent authorities on mariachi in the United States, a field that had been of little interest to scholars in Mexico.

Mariachi Uclatlán gradually morphed from a student ensemble to a professional group, but UCLA is still the center for mariachi graduate studies in the United States.

WHY DID MARIACHI MUSIC TAKE OFF IN THE UNITED STATES?

In 2008, it was estimated that one out of every five Mexican citizens lived in the United States. Culture has always flowed as freely back and forth across the U.S.-Mexico border as the shared population does. Mexicans have crossed over to work in the United States for as long as there has been a border. North Americans have traveled south to enjoy Mexico's charming, sunny, and affordable vacation spots, where they almost always heard mariachi music. Since most of the Southwest—Arizona, Texas, New Mexico, and California—used to be part of Mexico, the influence of culture and tradition also extends to music.

In the United States, among communities of Mexican origin, hiring mariachis follows the same patterns as in Mexico. However, these days, the group playing at a backyard party might be the student mariachi from a local school. They will earn the same pay as an adult mariachi, usually starting at about $300 an hour no matter the size of the group.

First-generation Mexican-American families fill with pride when their child plays with a mariachi; the sentiment and nostalgia runs deep, and the music connects them to home. Those families also have more disposable income than they had in Mexico and can more easily make the sacrifice to pay for instruments and lessons.

There are two big differences between students pursuing mariachi in the United States and those who pursue it in Mexico. First, unlike Mexico, in the United States, music education is available through public schools or after-school programs in many communities. If not totally free, it is usually within most parents' means. Second, Mexican-American children, as well as students of every other ethnicity, play mariachi music as an extracurricular activity, not as vocational training. Often the enrichment offered through membership in a mariachi, combined with the discipline and extra attention from directors, gives students a greater sense of belonging, a better attitude toward school, and pride in the way they view themselves and the Mexican culture. But few harbor dreams of making their living as a member of a mariachi group, as their peers might in Mexico.

HOMEGROWN MARIACHI EDUCATION IN MEXICO

In Mexico, the mariachi tradition is most often passed from father to son. A talented woman might become a ranchera singer, but there used to be virtually no opportunities for women to play in mariachi groups with men, and mixed groups were unheard of, largely because of social taboos.

Few working-class Mexicans could afford to send their children to music teachers, and among those that could, few would choose to have them educated as mariachis. Class-conscious middle-class families perceive mariachis as low status. They would consider the thought of educating their children to join a lower rank of society ridiculous, even though most Mexicans love mariachi music and see it as an important cultural symbol of their country.

The exceptions are the families of top mariachi groups, who understand the importance of good training. Even for poor mariachis, there was a free music conservatory in Mexico City and a folkloric conservatory in Guadalajara where students could study. Many of the best Mexican mariachis, men like Miguel Martínez, Antonio Hernández, Hector and Carlos Gama, Rigoberto Alfaro, Pepe Martínez, and Rafael Palomar (guitarist with Mariachi Vargas for twenty-five years), studied in music schools or conservatories at least long enough to sharpen their skills.

Raúl Ojeda, guitarronero with Mariachi Tenampa and teacher with the Mozart y Mariachi program in Santa Fe, New Mexico, tells the story of his education:

My father and grandfather were mariachis, and we moved around a lot so that my father's group

Mariachi Los Halcones de Cuba, Tonalá, Encuentro Internacional del Mariachi, 2007. Photo © 2009 Patricia Greathouse.

Raúl Ojeda, Mariscos la Playa, Albuquerque, 2008. Photo © 2009 Christopher Barnes.

Left to right: José Santiago, Francisco García, Elías Ojeda and Daniel Villa of Mariachi Tenampa serenade customers at their regular planta, Mariscos Altamar, in Albuquerque, New Mexico. Photo © 2009 Christopher Barnes.

could find work. I used to stand next to the guitarrón when his group played in the marketplace and listen to the sound. I loved the instrument.

There were twelve kids in our family, and I was the oldest boy. When I was fifteen, I was only in fourth grade and a lot bigger than the other kids. I told my dad I didn't want to go back to school. I was too embarrassed. My dad said, "Tomorrow, you're going to start guitar." He got Elías [Raúl's uncle who was his father's ward] and me up in the morning every day for six months straight, and we practiced, without stopping to eat, for six hours at a time.

He took us to his group and said, "I want my kids to start playing." The group said no, but he said, "You don't have to pay them. I just want them to stand in the group and feel the music." The band agreed, but pretty soon they changed their minds because we really couldn't play! The

practice went on, though, six hours a day. Soon they started coming to us and asking us how to play things. That felt good!

Ojeda's father also sent his children to solfège lessons, which was considered an important basis for any kind of music training. Solfège study is rare in the United States, but the best public school teachers emphasize note reading. In the classroom, it is important for mariachi students to read music so that they can learn pieces more quickly. It also enables teachers to work more easily with large groups of mixed instruments.

YOUTH EDUCATION IN THE UNITED STATES

Almost every public school mariachi class in the United States is mixed, and girls often outnumber boys. Only

Mark Fogelquist, Student Showcase, Mariachi Spectacular, Albuquerque, 2007. Photo © 2009 Christopher Barnes.

rarely do the students come from mariachi families.

José Santiago and Raúl Ojeda of Mariachi Tenampa teach for the Mozart y Mariachi program of the Santa Fe Youth Symphony as well as for the six conferences Tenampa gives a year. Santiago says,

[When I was young] not everyone could become a mariachi. My dad said you had to earn your traje. It was usually handed down from generation to generation. When I first started playing, I was one of three kids . . . in all of New Mexico learning mariachi, and all three of us were sons of mariachis. There were no school programs, there were no conferences. There was nothing like that.

I used to get laughed at. "Mariachi—Yah, ha, ha!" It didn't bother me because I was doing what I loved. Now do kids do that? No, it's, "You're in a mariachi! I want to do that!" It's like football.

In 1966, San Antonio music educator Belle San Miguel Ortiz began the first elementary school mariachi program in the nation. Since then, the movement has grown tremendously. These days, any student at a school with a mariachi program in the United States can sign up. The old prejudices that prevented women from joining groups are gone, and the elitist prejudice against mariachis themselves has been turned on its head. Students in traje are now proud of their heritage. Parents enthusiastically encourage their children to pursue mariachi music to the highest level. Tales of fist fights between parents over whose daughter or son gets to sing a solo are bandied about among directors, who occasionally ban difficult parents from participating in any mariachi functions.

In 2007, 2,200 public schools had mariachi programs. MENC's (Music Educators National Conference) Mariachi Board is made up of eminently qualified educators, including National Chair William Gradante, mariachi, educator,

Mozart y Mariachi violin class performs at Cinco de Mayo fundraiser, James A. Little Auditorium, Santa Fe, 2005. Photo © 2009 Christopher Barnes.

and historian; Mark Fogelquist, mariachi, ethnomusicologist, and educator; Mack Ruiz, Mariachi Cobre founding member and educator; Jonathan Clark, historian, educator, and mariachi; Laura Sobrino, mariachi, ethnomusicologist, and educator; and Noé Sánchez, mariachi music arranger and educator, among others. By providing professional support and training for teachers, the organization hopes to convey the importance of authentic mariachi education.

There are many outstanding mariachi programs and teachers in the United States. One of the best public school mariachi teachers in the United States, Mark Fogelquist, came to teaching after years of owning a mariachi restaurant and nightclub. After his Mariachi Uclatlán became highly successful, he and his brother followed the lead of other mariachis like Nati Cano and Pedro Rey Hernández, who had established their own restaurants as a showplace for their mariachis. Fogelquist's life was hard during those times.

In 1992, school administrators from Wenachee, Washington, in Los Angeles for a conference, came to see his show. In passing, they asked if he knew of a bilingual teacher who would be willing to relocate to Washington State. Fogelquist had a degree in Spanish, and he jumped at the chance to leave the restaurant business. In 1992, agricultural workers could get a green card if they had worked in the United States for ninety days. Suddenly Wenachee, a 100-percent, non-Spanish-speaking Anglo community, had an influx of Mexican immigrant children in the schools.

The first day of school, Fogelquist had thirty middle school students; some of the students had been in the

United States only twenty-four hours. When Fogelquist told them about his life as a mariachi, they were intrigued and Fogelquist started working with some of them after school. For Cinco de Mayo, they sang an out-of-tune version of "Las Mañanitas"; Fogelquist and his sixth-grade daughter Monica played first and second violin accompaniment, and the crowd went wild.

The administration agreed to fund a mariachi class if he could get fifteen students to sign up from the middle school and the high school across the street. Forty-seven students, from twelve to eighteen, enrolled in the class, and only one had ever played an instrument—an electronic keyboard.

In October of the first year, the principal asked them to play for the fall meeting with the Spanish-speaking parents, all of whom were farm workers. The students played "Volver, Volver (To Return, To Return)" and "Las Mañanitas (The Dear Mornings"—the Mexican celebration song) to a crowd of a hundred. Former attendance at the meeting had been only eight or nine; it became apparent that the key to getting Mexican parents involved in the school was mariachi music.

The program grew rapidly. Within a few years, Fogelquist's Mariachi Huenachi was one of the best student mariachis in the United States, winning two grand prize awards at the Mariachi Spectacular in Albuquerque.

Seeing the students learn was exciting for Fogelquist: "These were the poorest, the most humble people in the community, and it was the only thing that they had that represented them."

Silvia Vasquez Castro, Mozart y Mariachi Program, Santa Fe Youth Symphony Association. Photo © 2009 Christopher Barnes.

Fogelquist received the governor's Heritage Award for his contributions to the culture of Washington. Having taught in mariachi conferences since San Antonio in 1979, he started his own mariachi conference in Wenachee. Still going, the Northwest Mariachi Festival celebrated its tenth year in 2008. José Hernández and Mariachi Sol de Mexico came to Wenachee for the first conference, and Hernández invited Monica, a senior and Fogelquist's only child, to join his women's group, Mariachi las Reynas de Los Angeles (known as Mariachi Reyna). A former Suzuki violin student and a strong singer, Monica accepted and still performs with Mariachi Reyna.

Fogelquist was lured away from Washington State in 2001 by the Sweetwater School District in southern California, which serves 80,000 urban middle and high school students and was looking for someone to start their mariachi program.

Fogelquist's Mariachi Chula Vista is now the best mariachi, bar none, in the San Diego area. They practice daily and play over 200 times a year, all of which he attends. Their schedule has made them money, and in addition to buying beautiful custom-made trajes, Fogelquist takes the students on great trips. In 2007, they vacationed for several days in Puerto Vallarta before attending the Encuentro Internacional del Mariachi in Guadalajara.

A PRIVATE MARIACHI ACADEMY

The Academia Internacional de Mariachi de Valentin del Castillo in El Paso, Texas, successfully trains children from the age of three up in the music of Mexico. A private music school, it's also home to several youth performance groups.

Del Castillo was born in Ciudad Valles, San Luis Potosi, and raised in Mexico City. A third generation mariachi who has played with numerous elite groups, he has four brothers who are also mariachis. His own three children, two boys and a girl, perform in Mariachi Los Toritos, the top group of his academy. His beginning group, Mariachi Los Potrillos, may be the youngest performing mariachi in the world. Members range from three to ten years old.

NONPROFIT MARIACHI PROGRAMS

One of the biggest challenges for mariachi teachers is the violin section. Violins are hard to tune, even harder to play, and almost impossible for a beginner to produce a good sound on. To add to the difficulties, when the violins play with trumpets and an armonía section, they can't hear themselves well, and intonation and technique become a vague concept. The Mozart y Mariachi program of Santa Fe, New Mexico, avoids some of the initial problems by starting the violins alone. Students can borrow an instrument and receive scholarships based on need.

Initially dedicated to string orchestra instruments, mariachi became part of the program in 2002—it was a natural fit for the students and the instructors. Armonía and trumpet instruction were added to the curriculum; for violinists to enter the mariachi class, they had to finish Suzuki Book 1 and play a solo recital of the entire book by memory.

The beginning violin program is based on the Suzuki Method, a pedagogy popular around the world. Its students are a mix of ethnicities, and all communications are in both Spanish and English.

A student-mentor program recruits well-trained classical violin students from the Santa Fe Youth Symphony. Mozart y Mariachi's success is due in large part to the hard work and dedication of the nonprofit's governing board, which has made a commitment to raise funds to support scholarships and instrument rental. The Rotarians, who have dedicated themselves to providing trajes, instruments, and instruction at many of the public school programs in Santa Fe, raised money for the group's trajes.

Today, the violin classes are taught by trained Suzuki teachers who are also accomplished classical musicians. Mariachi Tenampa members José Santiago and Raúl

Gary Gonzales and Eddie Hernández of Mariachi Azteca, Cinco de Mayo fundraiser, Santa Fe, New Mexico, 2005. Fernando Romero on guitarrón. Photo © 2009 Christopher Barnes.

Ojeda, of Albuquerque, travel to Santa Fe two days a week to teach the mariachi classes. Both instructors are excellent musicians who bring the reality of life as professional mariachis to their teaching. Santiago says:

To really be a mariachi, you have to be able to accept a few things—number one, you are probably never going to be rich. You can make a very decent living at it . . . but you should have something to fall back on. It should come second to education, because it's very unpredictable. One month it could be great, or one year, or one season, others it could be very rough.

[Youth groups] have had an effect on the professional groups. . . . It's taken away business . . . because these groups now are able to market themselves very cheaply. And some of the kids can pull off a gig very well. Teaching and conferences are areas where professional groups aren't affected by youth groups.

Teaching is the direction where all the professional groups are heading, and that has been evident for the last ten years. Everybody's starting to quit their groups and go where the teaching is—in California, Texas, New Mexico, and even in Mexico.

CONFERENCES

Mariachi conferences have been the single biggest development in mariachi education in the United States. People of all ages and ability levels attend conferences across the country. Many professional mariachis spend a great deal of their time traveling to teach at conferences, where they give students a chance to see a level of musicianship they normally wouldn't.

Providing a three-day setting of fun, intense learning, and ultimately, exhaustion for teachers, sponsors, and students, conferences have given the mariachi education movement momentum and validation. At the end of the sessions, groups have an opportunity to showcase, each parading their unique colors, hairpieces, and musical accomplishments.

Directors love conferences because they inspire students and provide new repertoire that the director doesn't have to teach. Students come back from conferences with renewed desire to learn pieces they've heard in jam sessions (that often go until the wee hours of the morning). Cafeterias become places to gather to play and sing, and the best singers and players dazzle the beginners. Omar Olivas, formerly of Los Arrieros and now Mariachi Cobre's guitar player, says, "When I started out, I came to the Las Cruces conference. I was one of those kids who grew up in the conference, and now I'm back teaching here!"

Many mature men and women with jobs and families are attracted to conferences. They may feel bereft of a traditional culture and long for it. Trained to play violins, trumpets, or guitars as students, these older musicians attend, learn mariachi music, and often form groups. As Dan Sheehy said about his Mariachi Los Amigos, formed by people from varied cultural backgrounds, ". . . there was a sense of discovery, and placing themselves in the role of a mariachi musician was a little like trying on a different set of clothes; one that you liked the feel of, that looked good to you, and that seemed to have some intrinsic 'power' invested in it."

The opportunity for students to meet face to face and in the classroom the men and women who shaped the mariachi repertoire and made the classic recordings is awe inspiring. The older masters are unfailingly accessible, humble, and courteous. Being in a class with Miguel Martínez, Jesús Rodríguez de Híjar, or Rigoberto Alfaro teaching is the mariachi equivalent of a jazz trumpeter taking a workshop with Louis Armstrong.

The younger mariachi greats are awe inspiring, too. If the community volunteers are the engine that drives nonprofit conferences and the directors are the drivers, then top-notch mariachis are the navigators, offering direction and interpreting the signs along the way.

CONFERENCES IN THE UNITED STATES

SAN ANTONIO CONFERENCE

Josephine Ortega and her husband, Jesse, of San Antonio were vacationing in Cuernavaca when they heard a mariachi mass. They fell in love with it, came back home, and organized a group to perform the mass. The priest wouldn't initially let them play it in the main church, and they were assigned to a small chapel. However, the mass became so popular that soon they were back in the sanctuary of the church, singing five masses each Sunday.

The San Antonio conference evolved from that mariachi mass. When Mariachi Vargas arrived in San Antonio to

Los Arrieros, Las Cruces International Mariachi Conference, 2007. Photo © 2009 Christopher Barnes.

help with the conference in 1979, they were met by a large group of mariachis, all different ages and genders. Nothing in Mexico rivaled that conference; they were astonished and amazed. They didn't really know what to think of it. The San Antonio conference gradually faded with the rise of the Tucson conference.

TUCSON INTERNATIONAL MARIACHI CONFERENCE

In 1983, the Tucson International Mariachi Conference started and became popular almost immediately. The Tucson Conference, held in April of each year, has used both Mariachi Cobre and Mariachi Vargas as instructional staff. It is the biggest conference in the nation and has since turned more commercial in its interests and endeavors.

MARIACHI SPECTACULAR DE ALBUQUERQUE

The Albuquerque conference is one of the most inspiring conferences to attend. Founder and director Norberta Fresquez's commitment to bringing the giants of Mexican mariachi to her conference over the years has meant that members of groups like Mariachi Vargas, past and present, have made an impressive showing. Students love the chance to meet and interact with the mariachi legends.

It had always been Norberta Fresquez's dream to have a mariachi conference. When she was growing up in Deming, New Mexico, her family would gather around the radio each night to listen to the Spanish language station broadcast out of Mexico, which played mostly mariachi music. While the other kids went to the latest movies showing downtown, she took her twenty-five cents to see Miguel Aceves Mejía, Lucha Villa, and Vicente Fernandez in the Mexican movie theater.

When she moved to Albuquerque as a young woman, she couldn't believe how many mariachis there were—she was in heaven. She teamed with the dean of continuing education at the University of New Mexico for the first Mariachi

Spectacular, but split away from the college in 2001. In 2008, the Mariachi Spectacular enrollment neared 1,000 students from all over the west. According to Fresquez:

> We are the only conference who uses a large group of seasoned musicians to come up with our arrangements—people like Jesús Rodríguez de Híjar and Rigoberto Alfaro. There are more than thirty teachers who review the music and go over parts to make sure everything is correct. We also make sure that the teachers are acknowledged and respected. So many people who enjoy the music don't think beyond the recorded music or the singer to who was in back of the process, arranging, writing, and accompanying.

Fresquez also manages Mariachi Internacional Guadalajara, directed by German Gutierrez Corona, which travels extensively to perform and to teach at conferences. Fresquez's nonprofit organization produces *Mariachi Christmas* each December in Albuquerque. They bus in school children for four shows and provide teachers with curriculum so that the students learn about the instruments, traje de charro, and a little of the history of mariachi.

José Hernández has been an important part of the musical instruction at the Mariachi Spectacular for several years. Founder and musical director of Mariachi Sol de Mexico and the all-female Mariachi Reyna de Los Angeles, he also owns Cielito Lindo Restaurant in South El Monte, California, where both groups play regularly.

Born in Mexicali, Mexico, Hernández is a well-educated musician and a fifth-generation mariachi. A talented composer and arranger, his tunes perfectly capture the flavor of the Mexico. His mariachi travels extensively to perform and teach in conferences.

He maintains that mariachis can play any music as long as they play it mariachi style; he has also founded

Sol de Mexico Symphony Orchestra, which performed in Washington, D.C.

Hernández's Mariachi Heritage Society hires well-qualified mariachi instructors to educate school children in the greater Los Angeles area with the aim of teaching music and instilling pride.

LAS CRUCES INTERNATIONAL MARIACHI CONFERENCE

Phyllis Franzoy was on the Las Cruces Diocese Foundation board in 1988 when they were trying to find a fund-raiser that would reach into the community. That same year, she attended the Tucson Mariachi conference, which featured a concert by Linda Ronstadt and Mariachi Cobre.

She was enthralled. As a native of southern New Mexico, she's passionate about the traditional culture. About the founding of the Las Cruces International Mariachi Conference, she says:

It was divine intervention. I chewed on that idea like a dog with a bone. I knew we could do it if Tucson could do it! I brought the idea back to the diocese board. A former marine from New Jersey was director then, and his ideas clashed with mine—he wanted bagpipes in concert at Immaculate Heart Cathedral! Every meeting I would bring back my ideas and he would override them. I resigned. They called me back and asked

Roberto López (left), José Hernández (center), and Jesús Hernández (right) at Las Cruces International Mariachi Conference, 2007. Photo © 2009 Christopher Barnes.

me to be vice-president of the board. For the past ten years, the Diocese of Las Cruces has continued to present the conference.

Without a full-time director, Franzoy says it's a bit of a miracle that the November festival happens every year. Perhaps the fact that the Las Cruces conference is run by the diocese (there's a lot of praying going on) explains why it's grown to be one of the biggest and most popular conferences in the country.

A lone Mariachi Sol de Mexico trumpeter calls out during performance of "El Nino Perdido (The Lost Boy)" at the Las Cruces International Mariachi Conference, 2007. Photo © 2009 Christopher Barnes.

Mack Ruiz of Mariachi Cobre has heavily influenced the professionalism of their program, and Cobre has been at the helm of the education at Las Cruces since the beginning. "At Las Cruces, they give us the wheel," Ruiz says.

Franzoy looks at the impact the conference has on the community and the students, and she knows she has to keep the conference alive. Las Cruces is a small town with little access to corporate funding. Nonetheless, the local community comes out in force, and volunteers do almost all the work.

Mack Ruiz talks about Cobre's approach to education at conferences:

Robert Martínez and I wrote the curriculum for the conferences because we're the educators in the group. We wish all mariachi conferences had solid academic programming that parallels the standards for music education drafted by MENC, so that students will be learning many of the kinds of things that they would learn in a music class. We reinforce learning too—you'll see

instructors writing in class and introducing musical terms that students would learn in orchestra, band, or chorus. We teach history, and we teach theory.

SAN JOSÉ INTERNATIONAL MARIACHI FESTIVAL AND CONFERENCE

The San José Mariachi Conference was the brainchild of Stephen and Randy Carrillo's uncle, Tony Carrillo, who was a professor at San José State University. The first conference, held in 1991, was under the auspices of the Mexican Heritage Corporation, a non-profit organization.

The San José conference grew out of the Tucson conference and follows the same structure. Mariachi Cobre is the group in charge of the education, and the conference is small enough to be intimate.

The city of San José built the Mexican Heritage Center for the corporation, with the intention of supporting Hispanic culture. It is one of the largest multicultural art centers for Latinos in the United States. However, the Mexican Heritage Corporation is trying to balance the interests of other Mexican music and entertainment with that of mariachi, and the decisions have not always been in favor of mariachi music or local musicians. The conference and festival occurs in September; for concerts, big name singers and Latino groups make appearances along with mariachis like Cobre and Los Camperos. Linda Ronstadt has recently joined the artistic board, and many local groups feel left out.

ABOVE: Sergio Caratachea Alvarez, music director of Mariachi Internacional Guadalajara, San José International Mariachi Festival and Conference, San Jose, California, 2007. BELOW: Cristian Daniel López Cárdenas of Mariachi Internacional Guadalajara. Photos © 2009 Patricia Greathouse.

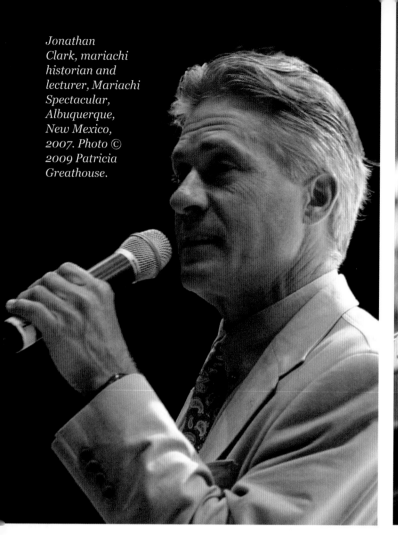

Jonathan Clark, mariachi historian and lecturer, Mariachi Spectacular, Albuquerque, New Mexico, 2007. Photo © 2009 Patricia Greathouse.

Jessica Garcia of Mariachi Son de México, El Paso, Texas. Photo © 2009 Christopher Barnes.

MARIACHI HISTORY CLASSES

Most educators and boards involved in mariachi conferences consider that one of their primary purposes is keeping and conveying mariachi culture. Every year, numerous conferences invite Jonathan Clark to lecture on different aspects of mariachi history. As the foremost expert on the history of the modern mariachi and a specialist on the history of Mariachi Vargas de Tecalitlán (in a field rife with misinformation and misunderstanding), Jon has gone a long way toward educating both students and performing mariachis. Having collected most of his information by conducting oral history interviews, his talks include not

only interesting anecdotes but also recordings, photos, and even film clips. Drawing from such a wealth of experience, he changes his class presentations continually.

Jon's interest in mariachi music began in 1975 while he was a guitar major at San José State University. He began playing guitar with Mariachi Aztlán, a fledgling mariachi group made up of students from different schools. They accompanied a ballet folklórico group named Los Lupeños de San José. After rehearsing somewhat unsuccessfully for several months without a guitarrón, out of desperation, Jon bought one and taught himself to play. In 1977, Los Lupeños received an invitation to perform at the Carnaval in Veracruz, and Mariachi Aztlán accompanied them.

After that engagement ended, Jon hitched a ride from Veracruz to Mexico City to check out Plaza Garibaldi. After receiving invitations to play there, the short story is that he stayed on in Mexico City and played guitarrón in and around Garibaldi for almost twelve years, learning about mariachi culture firsthand. He was the first and probably the only gringo crazy enough (in his words) to have done anything like that.

One day while attending a Mariachi Vargas rehearsal, Jon met the legendary Silvestre Vargas. As their friendship progressed, Jon realized that an incredible wealth of mariachi history would be lost when Vargas died, so he began to tape their conversations.

Jon says, "It was at that point I became a seat-of-the-pants mariachi historian." Since then, he has interviewed scores of seminal mariachi figures and recorded their testimonies for posterity. He has written many short articles, and hopes to publish a definitive book on the history of mariachi music.

MEXICO'S ENCUENTRO INTERNACIONAL DEL MARIACHI

The most extensive and far-reaching mariachi conference in the world is in Guadalajara, Jalisco. The impetus began after mariachis from Mexico like Jesús Rodríguez de Híjar and Mariachi Vargas de Tecalitlán began returning from teaching in conferences in the United States. They had experienced an interest level and an exuberance about learning mariachi music that didn't exist in Mexico. The whole concept of learning mariachi in an organized mass setting was new to them.

The Chamber of Commerce of Guadalajara, with the counsel and involvement of the veteran mariachis, began the Encuentro Internacional del Mariachi in 1993. Mariachi students and groups from around the globe travel to Guadalajara for the conference, and the conference, unlike others, sends student and professional groups to perform

Armando Cervantes Tinoco, Encuentro Internacional del Mariachi music director, 2007. Photo © 2009 Jasper Schriber.

in outlying communities for three weeks with concerts, parades, and classes the final week. About the Encuentro and the changes in mariachi education in Mexico, the conference's music director, Armando Cervantes Tinoco, a member of Mariachi Sol de América, says:

> [In my classes at the University of Guadalajara] the mariachi students are interested in learning to play in a very professional way because mariachi has become a career option.... We are pioneers in teaching mariachi music this way in Mexico.
>
> I am contributing *mi granito de arena* (my grain of sand), as we say in Mexico, to the talent, creativity, and heritage of our rich culture. We try to formalize our [mariachi] traditions a bit more than they were. In reality, [mariachi music is] one of the most interesting for many musicians because of the degree of difficulty, the beauty of the melodies, and the variety of repertoire. It continues to attract many musicians from diverse cultures to study here, at our mariachi conference. As

ambassadors for our culture, we carry our message of peace and brotherhood to the people of the world who invite us to perform for them out of love for our music.

The Encuentro is not just a grand celebration of the culture of western Mexico, it is an opportunity for promoting business and drawing tourists to Jalisco. Often the culture and the business are inextricably linked. A huge draw during the Encuentro, the Tequila Express takes tourists on a short ride from Guadalajara to the Herradura tequila plant.

Mariachis greet guests at the station, and as soon as the visitors board the train, drinks are available—anything from soda to aged tequila. In fact, for the price of the Tequila Express, there is as much food and drink as one wants to consume during the day.

Modern comfortable cars on the Tequila Express, where travellers are treated to mariachi music.
Photos © 2009 Patricia Greathouse.

THE FUTURE OF MARIACHI MUSIC

The future of mariachi music lies in the students that love mariachi. Now in classes, conferences, and learning from their elders, their fervor and desire hold great promise that mariachi will not only survive, but prosper.

ABOVE LEFT: Andrea Castro, Mozart y Mariachi Program, Santa Fe Youth Symphony Association, Santa Fe, New Mexico. Photo © 2009 Christopher Barnes. ABOVE RIGHT: Youngest member of Mariachi Los Potrillos, Academia Internacional de Mariachi de Valentin del Castillo, El Paso, Texas. Photo © 2009 Patricia Greathouse. LEFT: Mariachi Los Potrillos, Academia Internacional de Mariachi de Valentin del Castillo, El Paso, Texas. Photo © 2009 Patricia Greathouse.

RECIPES IN THE SPIRIT OF MARIACHI

Photo © 2009
Madeleine
de Sinety.
BELOW:
Photo ©
2009 Patricia
Greathouse.

Chile con Queso, Alcázar Bar–Style
(Alcazar Bar Chile and Cheese Appetizer)

The Alcazar Bar in Juarez was well known for its small mariachi ensemble and for this norteño melted cheese dish. My memory of the hot, delicious cheese filled with thick chile strips is inextricably linked with the sound of the little toupéed singer and "La Media Vuelta (The Half Turn)"—the Mexican song that most tugged at my heart strings when I was a student.

This is a delicious, sloppy appetizer, a kind of Mexican fondue. It bears almost no resemblance to the commercial product sold in the United States.

4 servings

2 tablespoons extra-virgin olive oil or vegetable oil

1 small onion, peeled, halved, and thinly sliced

$1/2$ teaspoon kosher salt, divided

5 chile poblanos (1 pound), roasted, peeled, seeded, and torn in strips

2 tomatoes, peeled, halved, and thinly sliced

1 garlic clove, minced

$3/4$ cup milk

2 cups grated asadero cheese, or Muenster (about $1/2$ pound)

Small handful of roughly chopped cilantro

Heat a 12-inch skillet until hot; add the oil. When it shimmers, add the onion and half the salt and sauté on medium heat until the onion is translucent and starting to brown. Add the chiles, tomatoes, garlic, and the rest of the salt. Sauté another 10 minutes, until mixture is heated through. The recipe may be stopped at this point and then refrigerated and reheated to finish right before serving.

To finish, add the milk to the chile mixture and bring to a boil. Add the cheese and stir until melted. Scatter cilantro over the top and serve immediately with a spoon and hot corn or flour tortillas or fresh crisp tortilla chips.

Photo © 2009
Christopher Barnes.

Guisado de Puerco

(Pork Ribs Braised in Roasted Tomato Salsa)

It's true that hunger makes the best sauce, but after making this dish numerous times, I have come to believe that the secret of this dish lies in the ingredients. Locally raised pork, garden tomatoes, onions, and fresh chiles roasted to intensify and soften the flavors, are stewed gently until you can suck the meat right off the bone. It is a magical combination, as are all simple dishes with the best ingredients.

Serves 4

PORK RIBS

5 pounds pork riblets or ribs, cut into individual
   pieces (have butcher saw long ribs in half)
Kosher salt
Freshly ground black pepper

ROASTED TOMATO SALSA

3–4 medium-size ripe tomatoes, about 1¹/₂ pounds
2 jalapeños, or more to taste
1¹/₂ onions, halved and peeled
¹/₂ teaspoon cumin
¹/₂ teaspoon Mexican oregano
2 garlic cloves, peeled and roughly chopped
2 tablespoons apple cider vinegar, as needed
2 cups water
2 bay leaves

Preheat the oven to 500 degrees F. (Convection works great for this recipe.) Rinse and dry the ribs with paper towels. Season generously with salt and pepper. Place the ribs in a large, shallow, flameproof casserole or roasting pan and place in the oven. Turn the ribs every 10 to 15 minutes so that they brown evenly and most of the fat cooks out of the meat. When the ribs are evenly browned (45 minutes to an hour), remove them from the pan and reserve. Pour off the grease and store in the freezer to use for tamales, if desired.

Lower the oven heat to 300 degrees F.

While the ribs are cooking, broil the tomatoes, jalapeños, and onions until the first side of the tomatoes blackens. (The jalapeños will broil more quickly than the other vegetables.) Turn the vegetables and continue to broil. Remove the jalapeños, and stem, peel, seed, and reserve. When the onions and the tomatoes blacken on the second side, remove them and place in a blender with the reserved jalapeños, cumin, oregano, and garlic cloves. Blend until smooth. Taste the salsa after blending, and add the vinegar if the mixture is too sweet or needs a little sparkle. Reserve.

Return the ribs to the pan and pour the reserved salsa and two cups water over the pork. Tuck the bay leaves into the sauce and cover the pan with aluminum foil. Bake in the oven for an hour or hour and a half, until the meat is tender but not falling off the bone.

The ribs may be made ahead to this point and refrigerated. To resume the recipe, remove any hardened fat that may have gathered on the top of the sauce or meat and discard it before warming the covered dish for an hour in a 325-degree F oven.

Serve hot in a bowl with some of the cooking juices and warm tortillas on the side.

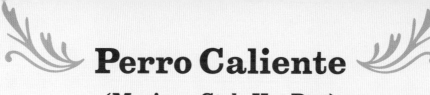

Perro Caliente
(Mexican-Style Hot Dog)

Hot dogs are common fast food in Mexico, and when they're prepared like this, they're fabulous. After you've had one, you'll never think about a wiener on a bun in the same way again—in fact, you may develop a craving and find yourself thinking about them all the time. The flavor of the bacon, heat and crunch of the salsa, and richness of the crema put them right over the top!

4 hot dogs
4 slices bacon
4 buns, split ¾ of the way through

GARNISHES

Mayonnaise, optional
Mustard, optional
Ketchup, optional
1 recipe Pico de Gallo (page 152)
12 slices pickled jalapeño
Crema

Wrap a slice of bacon around each hot dog from tip to tail. Secure with a toothpick if necessary. Grill over a flame or griddle in a skillet until bacon is crisp and golden all over and the hot dog has puffed up a bit. Briefly toast the buns without breaking them apart.

Slather buns with mayonnaise, mustard, and/or ketchup if desired. Arrange two spears of pickled jalapeño alongside the dog. Heap salsa into the buns, and snuggle the dogs in. Drizzle with crema.

*Photo © 2009
Christopher Barnes.*

Lomo de Puerco

(Carnitas-Style Pork Roast: Well-Seasoned, Crisp and Tender)

Pork is the most popular meat in Mexico, and carnitas are one of the most delicious ways of preparing it. A specialty of Jalisco, carnitas are sold out of carts on the street, in restaurants, butcher shops, and in groceries, where it's possible to ask for an order as you like it—with fat or without. Wrapped in soft corn tortillas and topped with salsa, they are heavenly.

Although carnitas are made commercially by rendering a whole hog in a huge iron kettle and finishing it by browning the meat in its own fat, some carnitas are prepared in a steamer so that they are soft and moist.

This roast is excellent for any occasion that calls for a satisfying meat dish or a well-seasoned filling for antojitos. When it comes out of the oven and we begin to cut it up, everyone snatches the choicest browned bits—it's irresistible!

Serves 8-10 as tacos, 4-6 as a main course roast

> 4 pounds boneless pork shoulder roast
>
> 2 tablespoons kosher salt (use half as much if substituting table salt)
>
> 4 tablespoons chile caribe (dried New Mexican red chile flakes; substitute any large chile flakes, and vary amounts depending on the heat of the chile)
>
> Mexican oregano, to taste

The day before serving, sprinkle the pork roast all over with salt, chile caribe, and oregano and refrigerate overnight.

Remove the pork from the refrigerator 2 hours before roasting to let it come to room temperature.

Three hours before serving, preheat the oven to 400 degrees F. (It's a good idea to use an oven thermometer—too hot an oven will ruin the roast.)

When the oven is hot, put the meat in a shallow pan fat side up and roast it for 2 hours in the middle of the oven. Take the pan out of the oven and turn the roast over carefully. Roast for 20 minutes more, then take the pan out of the oven and let the meat rest for 10 minutes, tented. Roughly chop it up into small chunks and put it on a warm platter to serve. Strain the fat, refrigerate, and save it for tamales or other savory recipes calling for lard.

Tacos de Lomo de Puerco con Piña

(Roast Pork Tacos with Grilled Pineapple)

These tacos are a delicious interpretation of the tacos al pastor that are cooked on a vertical rotisserie in Mexico. The crunchy moist pork, hot smoky chipotle chiles, fruity-tart pineapple, cilantro, onion, and crema combine to deliver unforgettable flavor. Preparing and cooking the meat couldn't be easier. Make the barbecue salsa and crema ahead of time, put the roast in the oven, put the pineapple on the grill while you make the cilantro, onion, and serrano fresh salsa, and heat up the tortillas. Invite guests to assemble the tacos themselves and add condiments to taste. Serve with Frijoles Borrachos (page 161) and Grilled Corn (page 66) on the side.

Serves 8

1 recipe Carnitas-Style Pork
    Roast (page 147)
36 fresh corn tortillas
1 each of the recipes that follow

While the roast is resting, warm the tortillas individually on a comal or in a skillet. Keep them warm in a clean folded dishtowel.

Carve pork into bite-size chunks and arrange on a platter. Serve tacos with the grilled pineapple, chipotle salsa, cilantro, onion, and serrano salsa, and crema on the side.

Tacos al Pastor. Photo © 2009 Christopher Barnes.

CREMA
(THICKENED MEXICAN CREAM —CRÈME FRAÎCHE)

Ubiquitous in Mexico, crema is invaluable as a topping for many antojitos and desserts. It's simple to make and far better than the bottled products on the market.

$^1/_2$ pint unpasteurized heavy cream
$^1/_4$ cup cultured buttermilk or plain cultured yogurt
The morning of the day before serving, combine the cream and the buttermilk or yogurt in a glass jar. Let rest in a very warm location for at least 12 hours, or until the cream thickens. Refrigerate. The cream will thicken more in the refrigerator. It keeps well.

SALSA DE BARBACOA CON CHIPOTLE
(CHIPOTLE BARBEQUE SAUCE)

A powerful sauce that goes well on pork or grilled chicken, this concoction is not traditional; rather, it's a hybrid of Mexican and American barbecue flavors with a sharp chile bite.

$^1/_2$ ounce dried chipotle chiles (about 5), stemmed
    (use fewer for a milder sauce)
1 cup hot water
1 medium white onion, halved, and peeled
$^1/_2$ cup apple cider vinegar
$^1/_2$ cup firmly packed brown sugar
3 garlic cloves, peeled
$^1/_4$ cup extra-virgin olive oil
1 teaspoon kosher salt (or $^1/_2$ teaspoon table salt)
1 (14.5-ounce) can fire-roasted diced tomatoes

Put the chiles in the blender and cover with the water. Let soak 10 minutes, and then strain the chiles, reserving the water. Add the rest of the ingredients to the chiles and blend well, adding some of the reserved soaking water if needed.

Place the sauce in a nonreactive saucepan and bring to a boil. Simmer for 10–20 minutes, stirring occasionally. The sauce is finished when it thickens slightly and begins to look glossy. Let cool and use immediately or cover and refrigerate. It keeps a long time.

PIÑA A LA PARILLA
(GRILLED PINEAPPLE)

Intense, ripe pineapple is one of the true pleasures of a trip to Mexico. It adds zest and flavor to barbecued meats, and it's a snap to prepare. It's excellent slipped into tacos, and essential with Carnitas-Style Roast Pork Tacos.

  1 large ripe pineapple
  Vegetable oil

Heat the grill to medium-high and scrape clean. Cut the ends off the pineapple, then the skin, including the eyes. Stand the pineapple on end and cut in quarters lengthwise. Remove the core from each of the pieces and then cut each quarter in thirds lengthwise to make spears.

Brush the pineapple spears with oil. Oil the grill using a crumpled paper towel moistened with the cooking oil and held with a pair of tongs. Lay the pineapple on the grill. Cook until it has deep grill marks and has become a deeper yellow color. Turn and repeat on the second side.

Remove pineapple from the grill. To serve, cut into bite-size pieces and serve warm or at room temperature.

SALSA FRESCA DE CILANTRO
(CILANTRO, ONION, AND SERRANO FRESH SALSA)

My first memory of eating this salsa was over twenty years ago. We were traveling back home from the Pacific coast, it was late, and we were tired. Just off the peripheral highway that runs around Guadalajara, we could see faraway vendors at a crossroads illuminated by bare bulbs strung from nearby utility poles.

Outfitted from head to toe in brilliant spotless white and wearing a small white cap, the vendor we chose looked like a Mexican version of Louisiana chef Paul Prudhomme. His tacos al pastor were irresistible, cooked on a vertical rotisserie and served in tiny double soft corn tortillas. He loaded them up with meat and this fresh salsa. We gave one plate to our sleepy children, and for the next fifteen minutes, we passed plates into the car as the children devoured tacos. When we got our turn, we ate twice as many as we thought we would; they were the most delicious we had ever tasted.

It's essential to make this salsa right before serving because it will lose its crunch and freshness. Likewise, the cilantro needs to be chopped by hand. It makes a good match with any cooked salsa, adding just a bit more punch, texture, and flavor. Omit the chile to serve with other hot salsas.

  1 serrano chile, stemmed, seeded, and minced
    (optional)
  1 large bunch fresh cilantro, finely chopped
  1/2 white onion, peeled and finely chopped
  1/2–3/4 teaspoon kosher salt
  1 tablespoon water
  Juice of half a lime

Combine all ingredients in a nonreactive bowl, mix well, and serve immediately.

Pozole Rojo con Lomo de Puerco

(Dried Corn and Red Chile Stew with Crispy Pork Roast)

A delicious, savory, big-kernel corn stew, pozole makes an excellent dish for a party; there's little last-minute preparation and everyone loves it. Although traditional both in Mexico and the Southwest ("pozole" is spelled "posole" in the United States), this recipe is singular. Its provenance is a combination of memory and desire: a childhood friend's old Texas grandmother used to make a posole similar to this, and her version is my all-time favorite. I have combined it with the satisfying richness of salty roast pork rather than the soft stewed pork that normally flavors the dish.

This version is more highly flavored than the traditional posole of northern New Mexico, which is a very plain stew of corn and pork, using neither chile nor tomato. Mexican cooks wouldn't use canned tomatoes, but the Texas grandmother did, and it works well in this recipe. Mexicans serve sliced radishes, chopped cabbage or lettuce (considered more refined), chopped onion, dried oregano, avocado, and lime on the side. Each can be added to taste to individual bowls. The salty, golden melting meat of the roasted pork goes very well with the fresh crunch of the vegetables. Together, they make a sort of soup and salad combo in a bowl. Start the recipe a day before serving—in fact, everything except roasting the pork can be done ahead of time.

Serves 12–15

1 recipe Carnitas-Style Pork Roast (page 147), prepared so that it comes out of the oven just before serving the pozole

12 cups pork broth (make by simmering 2 pounds pork neck bones in lightly salted water for an hour), chicken stock, or water (for a vegetarian version, omit the pork roast and use water to cook the pozole)

1 (32-ounce) package frozen pozole*, rinsed and drained several times

2 bay leaves

1 tablespoon kosher salt (or 1¹/₂ teaspoons table salt)

1¹/₂ large onions, quartered

8 large garlic cloves, peeled and chopped

4 dried New Mexico red chiles, stemmed and seeded, more to taste (or substitute ancho chiles)

1 teaspoon Mexican oregano

2 (14-ounce) cans tomatoes with juice

2 tablespoons extra-virgin olive oil

*Sold fresh or frozen in tortilla shops, Mexican grocery stores, and supermarkets in the Southwest, pozole may be labeled maiz *nixtamalado* or *nixtamal*. In areas where it is impossible to find pozole, hominy may be substituted, but the texture is overcooked for this dish, so it should be drained and added after the broth has been simmered for an hour.

GARNISHES

4 cups thinly shredded green cabbage cut in 1-inch lengths

5 scallions, sliced, or ¹/₂ cup chopped yellow onion

4–5 radishes, thinly sliced

2 avocados, cut in large dice (prepare the avocado right before serving)

1 bunch cilantro, chopped

Dried Mexican oregano

Lime sections

Photo © 2009
Christopher Barnes.

Pour 12 cups of pork broth, stock, or water and pozole into an 8-quart stew pot. Add the bay leaves and salt. Bring the liquid to a boil and then lower the heat to maintain a simmer. Skim off any foam that rises to the top.

Put the onion, garlic, red chiles, oregano, and tomatoes in a blender and process until fairly smooth. Add to the stew pot. Add the olive oil and simmer for another hour or two, or until the flavors meld and the posole "blooms" and is tender. Add more water as needed as the stew cooks to maintain plenty of broth.

When the posole is tender, taste for seasoning and add more salt to taste.

Ladle hot posole into individual bowls and offer the cabbage, scallions, radishes, avocado, cilantro, oregano, and lime on the side for each person to add to the bowl at the table, along with pieces of roast pork.

Photo © 2009
Christopher Barnes.

Tacos de Arrachera con Pico de Gallo

(Grilled Steak Tacos with Fresh Tomato, Jalapeño, Cilantro, and Onion Salsa)

Arrachera is a common cut of beef in Jalisco—inexpensive, fast cooking, and delicious. Seasoning the steak ahead of time adds great savor to the meat, and the addition of a fresh salsa, called salsa mexicana, salsa fresca, or pico de gallo—depending on where you are in Mexico—adds a zesty counterpunch to the beef's robust flavor. Serve with a dollop of guacamole, shredded cabbage, and a squeeze of lime. Small bowls of frijoles borrachos are a great side to the tacos.

Serves 2–4

THE ARRACHERA

1 pound skirt steak or thin flank steak

Olive or vegetable oil

Kosher salt and freshly ground black pepper, to taste

8 corn tortillas

PICO DE GALLO (SALSA FRESCA)

1 cup chopped ripe red tomatoes (for best flavor in winter, substitute ¹/₂ pint cherry tomatoes)

1–2 fresh jalapeños, stemmed, seeded, and chopped

1 small onion, chopped

Handful of cilantro, chopped

1–2 tablespoons apple cider vinegar or lime juice

¹/₂ teaspoon kosher salt

Grilled arrachera for tacos. Photo © 2009 Christopher Barnes.

*Pico de gallo.
Photo © 2009
Christopher
Barnes.*

Pat the steak dry and rub with olive oil. Salt and pepper generously. Refrigerate overnight.

Make a medium-hot charcoal fire in the grill, or heat a gas grill to medium-high. When the fire is so hot that you can't hold your hand 6 inches above the heat for more than 3 seconds, scrape the grate clean and coat liberally with an oiled paper towel, held in tongs.

While the fire is heating up, make the salsa fresca by combining all the ingredients and 2 tablespoons water. Mix gently. Taste and add more salt, vinegar, or lime juice to taste.

Put the steak on the grill for a minute, then quickly turn it 180 degrees to create hatch marks. Let steak cook another 2 minutes or so, depending on the thickness, then turn it over and repeat.

After the second side has cooked for 3 minutes, check the interior temperature of the meat by cutting into it with a sharp knife. An arrachera is best medium rare, as it tends to toughen when cooked longer.

Take the steak off the grill and let rest on a warm plate, tented with foil, for 5 minutes while you warm the tortillas.

Heat a frying pan or comal and moisten it with a little oil. Place a tortilla on the oil, rubbing it around so that the oil gets distributed, then turn the tortilla over. Cook on both sides briefly, until the tortilla begins to puff in spots. Tuck into a clean kitchen towel to reserve, and repeat with the remaining tortillas.

When all the tortillas are heated up, slice the steak as thinly as possible, distribute the meat among the tortillas, and serve with the salsa and lime sections.

Torta Ahogada

(Mexican Dip Sandwich)

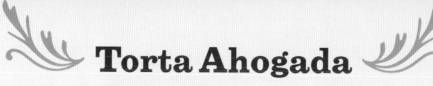

This scrumptious Mexican sandwich is similar to a French dip. The melting tenderness of a slowly braised roast is ratcheted up by slow cooking in roasted tomatoes, onions, and jalapeño. The best roasts for braising are those with lots of connective tissue and fat—in other words, pieces of meat that are economical and full of flavor. Put the meat on low to cook slowly all night, and in the morning, the house will be filled with fragrant aromas.

Serves 8–12

Photo © 2009 Christopher Barnes.

- 3–4 pounds braising roast (chuck or pork shoulder is excellent, or substitute other roast appropriate for moist slow cooking), trimmed of excess fat and rinsed well
- 1 recipe Roasted Tomatoes, Onions, and Jalapeños (page 155)
- 2 quarts beef broth or combination beef and chicken broth
- 1 tablespoon salt
- 1 fresh telera roll (soft Mexican sandwich roll) or hoagie bun per person
- Cebolla en Escabeche (Pickled Onions) (page 155)
- Finely shredded green cabbage
- Lime

Place the trimmed roast in a slow cooker and cover with the Roasted Tomatoes, Onions, and Jalapeños and the beef broth. Add the salt and turn the cooker to low. Cook for 8 hours, or overnight, until the meat is fork-tender and separates easily. Alternatively, cook in a 275-degree F oven for 5–6 hours in a stew pot with a tight-fitting lid. Replenish liquid with water as necessary.

Cool to lukewarm, drain meat, and discard fat and obvious connective tissue. Cut the meat into 1/3- to 1/2-inch pieces across the grain. It's fine if the meat falls apart. If serving immediately, skim fat from the liquid and discard, put the meat back into the sauce, and reheat. If serving later, put the meat back into the liquid and refrigerate. Remove hardened fat and gently reheat meat in the liquid before serving.

Split the rolls and arrange a generous quantity of meat on the bottom half of each sandwich. Ladle sauce over the inside of the sandwich, then put the top half on and ladle sauce over that. Serve immediately with Pickled Onions, shredded cabbage dressed with a little salt and lime juice, and Mexican-Style Grilled Corn (page 66).

Cebolla en Escabeche

(Pickled Onions)

These delicious onions are the backbone of Mexican condiments. I always have a jar on hand. They're also very good in a salad with butter lettuce, avocado, and jicama.

Photo © 2009 Christopher Barnes.

1 large red onion, cut in rounds 1/8-inch thick
1/2 cup apple cider vinegar
1/2 cup water
1/2 teaspoon salt
1/2 teaspoon sugar
1 bay leaf

Place all ingredients in a noncorrosive saucepan.

Bring to a simmer and cook until onions begin to turn translucent, 10–12 minutes. Cool, then store in a glass jar in the refrigerator. They keep a long time.

Roasted Tomatoes, Onions, and Jalapeños

7 medium-size ripe tomatoes (out of season, hothouse tomatoes will do)
1–2 jalapeños, plus more to taste
1 1/2 onions, peeled and halved
2 garlic cloves
2 tablespoons apple cider vinegar, optional
Salt to taste

Broil the tomatoes, jalapeños, and onions until they blacken, then turn and blacken the other side. (The jalapeños will broil more quickly than the tomatoes and onions.) Remove the jalapeños; peel, seed, and reserve. Place the tomatoes, jalapeños, onions, and garlic cloves in a blender. Blend until smooth. Taste and add up to 2 tablespoons of vinegar if the sauce is too sweet. Pour into a bowl and reserve; heat before serving.

Pollo Enchilado

(Chicken Breasts with Ancho and Chipotle Chile Rub)

Roasted, grilled, fried, in soup, or as a filling for tacos or tamales, chicken is one of the most common sources of protein on the Mexican table. This is a fabulous, simple dish for entertaining that can be easily expanded.

Curing chicken with salt and sugar seasons the meat all the way to the bone and improves the juiciness and texture too. Kosher salt is pure salt designed for koshering meats. Its large flakes make it easy to see when sprinkling on a dish or seasoning meat or poultry. It's also excellent for sauces and stews.

Following this recipe precisely produces perfectly seasoned and moist $1\frac{1}{4}$-pound chicken breasts, which may be cut in half for smaller servings. For breasts that weigh less, the easiest way to assure perfect cooking is to use a roasting or quick-read thermometer and reduce the cooking time.

Serve chicken with roasted potatoes dressed with a cilantro pesto or a side of puréed potatoes.

Serves 6–12, depending on appetites

CHILE RUB

2 tablespoons kosher salt (or substitute 1 tablespoon table salt)

$\frac{1}{4}$ cup brown sugar

1 whole ancho chile, stemmed, seeded, rinsed, dried, and torn or cut into small pieces

1 dried chipotle chile, stemmed, seeded, rinsed, dried, and torn or cut into small pieces

1 teaspoon whole cumin seeds, toasted in a dry pan until fragrant

3 cloves garlic, peeled and coarsely chopped

1 teaspoon Mexican oregano

6 pounds chicken breasts, wings attached, each weighing $1\frac{1}{4}$ pounds, or equal weight chicken quarters

Combine the salt, sugar, chiles, cumin, garlic, and Mexican oregano in a food processor. Pulse until everything is minced.

Rub the breasts all over with the mixture. Refrigerate overnight.

Preheat the oven to 425 degrees F. Remove chicken from the refrigerator and arrange in a single layer on a rack set over a shallow rimmed baking pan. For 1¹/₄-pound breasts, roast about 45–50 minutes, or until an instant-read thermometer registers 155 degrees F when inserted into the thickest part of the meat. (Reduce the cooking time for smaller pieces, and cook to an internal temperature of 155 degrees F. Cook quarters to 165 degrees F.)

Let chicken rest for ten minutes before serving. During the rest, the chicken will come up to 165 degrees F for breasts or 175 degrees F for quarters, and the juices will disperse into the meat instead of running out when the chicken is cut. Serve chicken with Papas de Lima y Cilantro (page 159) or with roasted or puréed potatoes.

Photo © 2009
Christopher Barnes.

Birria

(Tender Jalisco-Style Steamed Meat and Red Chile Stew)

One of the most popular dishes in Guadalajara, birria is meat marinated in chiles and spices and tender-cooked. The meat is served in its savory juices. Huge outdoor restaurants dedicated to its preparation and consumption line the highway to the airport in Guadalajara, complete with mariachis for hire.

For a party, increase the amounts proportionally and use 2 or 3 steamers. Begin marinating the meat the day before serving.

Serves 6

3 1/2 pounds pork shoulder roast, lamb shoulder roast, goat, beef chuck roast, short ribs, baby back ribs, or a combination

2 teaspoons kosher salt (for meat)

5 cascabel chiles, seeded and stemmed

3 ancho chiles, seeded and stemmed

3 guajillo chiles, seeded and stemmed

2 garlic cloves, whole and unpeeled

1 teaspoon whole cumin seeds

1/2 teaspoon whole black peppercorns

2 tablespoons cider vinegar

3 cups water, plus more for steaming, divided

2 pounds Roma tomatoes

2 pounds small potatoes, peeled and cut into large pieces

One recipe Cilantro, Onion, and Serrano Salsa made without chile if desired (see page 149)

Lime wedges

Rinse the meat under cold running water, dry, and salt liberally on all sides. Reserve. (This step may be done 24 hours before the next step; refrigerate the meat.)

Toast the chiles, garlic, cumin, and pepper on a comal or in a hot skillet for a few minutes, turning the chiles and garlic frequently and shaking the skillet to move the spices around. When the chiles change color, take the garlic out and peel it. Put everything into the blender with the vinegar and water. Blend until the mixture is liquid with no large pieces.

Spread the chile mixture over the meat and refrigerate overnight.

Four hours before serving, set up a collapsible steamer in a large, heavy stew pot with a tight-fitting lid. Add 2 cups water to the bottom of the pot. Load the meat evenly into the steamer, cover, and bring to a boil. Lower heat and steam for 2 to 3 hours, replenishing water as necessary. Steam until the meat is completely tender.

Meanwhile, broil tomatoes until blackened on both sides. Purée in a blender and reserve.

Cook potatoes in heavily salted water until just tender. Drain and reserve.

Remove meat carefully from steamer. Pour liquid from the bottom of the steamer into a bowl and skim off the fat.

Photo © 2009
Patricia Greathouse.

(Reserve stew pot without cleaning.) Measure the liquid and add enough water to make 2 cups. Put liquid into the stew pot with the puréed tomatoes, taste for seasoning, and add salt if needed.

Separate meat, fat, and bones if necessary (leave ribs intact if desired) and reserve. Combine sauce and tomatoes in the stew pot. Bring to a boil and add meat and potatoes. Stir gently until heated through. Serve hot with Cilantro, Onion, and Serrano Salsa, hot corn tortillas, and lime wedges.

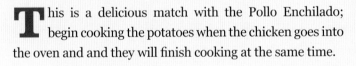

Papas de Lima y Cilantro

(Golden Potatoes with Cilantro Lime Salsa)

This is a delicious match with the Pollo Enchilado; begin cooking the potatoes when the chicken goes into the oven and and they will finish cooking at the same time.

> 2 pounds egg-sized golden potatoes (some brands are marketed simply as "gold"; others as Yukon Gold or Yellow Finn)
> 1 tablespoon kosher salt (or substitute 1^1/$_2$ teaspoons table salt)

Scrub the potatoes. Put them in a 2- or 3-quart pot, cover with water, and add the salt. Bring to a boil, then cover and turn heat down to maintain a simmer. Cook until a knife easily pierces all the way through a test potato. Drain, then return potatoes to pot and shake gently over heat until they are dry. Put in a serving dish and dress with Cilantro Lime Salsa. Serve immediately.

CILANTRO LIME SALSA

An addictive-tasting silky sauce that's also great on fish or meat, this salsa is similar to a pesto without the nuts. Leave the lime juice out until the last minute because it will turn the cilantro a dull color if added ahead of time. Add a jalapeño for a spicy kick if you like.

> 1 bunch cilantro, rinsed and dried
> 3 medium cloves garlic, peeled and sliced
> ^{1}/$_2$ teaspoon salt
> ^{1}/$_2$ cup extra-virgin olive oil
> 1^1/$_2$ tablespoons freshly squeezed lime juice (from ^{1}/$_2$ of a large, juicy lime)

Put all ingredients except the lime juice into a blender jar. Pulse until ingredients begin to move easily and then blend continuously until the mixture is very smooth. Add the lime juice right before serving and mix well.

Frijoles

(Beans)

Beans have been one of the essential foods of Mexico for thousands of years; combined with the slaked corn of tortillas, they make a complex protein. Mexican beans come in many delicious varieties, and any could be used in the recipes below. If you love beans and haven't tried pinquitos or peruanos, please do. See Resources (page 172).

Basic Beans

Beans are best cooked in a clay cooking pot. I often cook beans in a pressure cooker for 45 minutes when I'm in a hurry, and then finish them by simmering for 20–30 minutes. Beans cook at different rates depending on their age and dryness, so be patient and give them as long as it takes. There is no such thing as a bean that won't get soft, and contrary to a misguided trend, crunchy beans are not ideal—they're hard to digest and don't taste good. The best beans are cooked until soft with a thick gravy—the ultimate comfort food.

Yields about a quart

- 2 cups pinto beans, pinquitos, bolita beans, peruanos, or other
- 2 bay leaves
- 1 small onion, chopped
- 1 large garlic clove, peeled but left whole (It should dissolve in cooking—if not, mash it with a spoon before serving.)
- 2 teaspoons kosher salt

Pick through the beans to remove any stones, odd seeds, or tiny dirt clods. Rinse the beans very well and drain. Discard any beans that float.

Put the beans in a 3-quart saucepan and add water, covering beans by 1 1/2 inches. Add bay leaves, onion, and garlic and bring the water to a boil. (Do not add the salt at this point!) Reduce heat and simmer until beans are tender, which might take several hours.

Add boiling water as needed. (Although there are several tests for determining if beans are tender, the simplest method is to taste one. It should be soft enough to provide little resistance.) After the beans are tender, add the salt and cook until sauce has thickened. Remove bay leaves before serving. Serve them hot or cool beans to room temperature and then refrigerate.

Frijoles Refritos

(Refried Beans)

Beans are most often served refrito (well fried) in Mexico, and refritos are used for fillings in many antojitos. Enriched with lard and mashed to a paste, they come on the side of many dishes sprinkled with a little cheese. Any fat may be substituted for the lard, but the flavor will not be authentic. Use your judgment when it comes to the lard—Mexicans, who are fond of the flavor, use more than most North Americans are comfortable with.

Serves 2

1/2 small onion, peeled and chopped
2 cups beans with broth
2 tablespoons good-quality lard or bacon grease

Heat the lard in a skillet and add the onion. Sauté until onion is translucent and then add half the beans. Heat and mash the beans, gradually cooking the broth away. Add more beans and repeat. Beans are finished when they are dry enough to hold their shape on a spoon.

Frijoles Borrachos

(Drunken Beans)

This is one of my favorite dishes—the Mexican version of baked beans, although they aren't at all sweet. Sometimes they are served with cut-up hot dogs—how would you say "beanie weenies" in Spanish? Leave out the beer, and this recipe becomes frijoles charros, cowboy beans. Serve them as a separate soup course drizzled with crema* or in a bowl as a savory side to any kind of main course. Make them a day ahead to let the flavors meld.

Yields 1 1/2 quarts

1 recipe Basic Beans, thoroughly cooked
1 bottle Mexican beer
3 ounces chorizo, crumbled
1/2 cup chopped smoky bacon (freezing the bacon

*Crema is a mild, slightly thickened cultured cream commonly used in Mexican cooking. Sour cream is substituted in many restaurants in the United States, but it isn't the same. See page 148 for a simple recipe for making crema.

makes it easier to chop)
1 tomato, chopped
1 jalapeño, stemmed, seeded, and chopped
1/2 white onion, chopped fine
1 clove garlic, minced

Add the beer to the beans and simmer while you prepare the rest of the ingredients.

Sauté the chorizo in a skillet over medium heat. Remove from skillet and reserve. Cook the bacon in the same skillet until it begins to brown and releases most of its fat. Add chorizo and bacon (along with the grease, for extra flavor) to beans along with the tomato, jalapeño, onion, and garlic.

Cook gently for at least 30 minutes, stirring occasionally and adding a little more water as needed. Serve when the flavors are well blended, or cool and refrigerate. Beans are always better the second day.

Machaca Burrito

These delicious burritos are a bit like beef stew wrapped in a tortilla.

This machaca also makes a great bowl of green chile with the tortilla served alongside.

Yeilds 12–15 burritos

> 2 tablespoons olive oil
> 3 pounds beef chuck bone-in roast, rinsed and dried
> 1 large onion, chopped
> 3 cloves garlic, peeled and chopped
> 1 green bell pepper, chopped
> 3 ribs celery, sliced
> 1–2 pints frozen green chile, to taste
> 1 (28-ounce) can diced tomatoes, broken up
> 1 tablespoon kosher salt
> Freshly ground black pepper
> 3–4 large russet potatoes, peeled and cubed, or 1 quart cooked Basic Beans (page 160)

Heat oil in a stew pot. When it shimmers, add the roast and brown on all sides. Take the meat out of the pot and reserve it on a plate. Add the onion, garlic, bell pepper, and celery to the pot, salt lightly, and sauté until the onion is transparent. Add the chiles, tomatoes, salt, pepper, and reserved roast and cover completely with water.

Partially cover the pot and bring the liquid to a boil. Lower the heat and simmer the roast until the meat is falling off the bone. (A true simmer, with the lid propped open, should barely bubble.) It will take several hours. Alternatively, cook the ingredients in a pressure cooker until tender, 35–45 minutes.

Take the roast out of the broth and let it cool. Skim the fat off the broth and add the potatoes or beans and cook until the potatoes are tender and the broth has thickened a bit (add more water if needed). Shred the meat with a fork, discarding the fat and bone. Put the meat back in the broth and bring to a boil. Add salt to taste if needed. Serve immediately in a bowl or use to fill burritos.

FOR THE BURRITOS

> Flour tortillas, one per person, heated through on a griddle or wrapped in aluminum foil and warmed in the oven
> Plenty of Monterey jack or medium cheddar cheese, grated

Using a slotted spoon, arrange the machaca filling down the middle of a hot tortilla, leaving space on both ends to fold it over. Sprinkle cheese on top of the meat to taste. Fold up both ends of the burrito to keep the juices from running out. Roll up the burrito and place seam side down on a plate. Serve immediately. To transport the burritos, wrap tightly in foil, leaving one end easy to open.

Flan de Naranja

(Orange Flan)

Flan is the unofficial national dessert of Mexico, found in every corner of the country. A simple custard, it makes a lovely caramel syrup while it cooks that sets it apart from nursery food. It's particularly good for a special dinner because you can make it a day ahead of time.

If possible, use an organically raised orange to avoid the chemical residues on the peel, or scrub the skin with a drop of detergent and hot water and rinse thoroughly.

Serves 6–8

> $3/4$ cup sugar
> 2 cups whole milk (or substitute 2-percent milk)
> Zest of 1 orange
> 5 egg yolks
> 1 whole egg
> 1 (14-ounce) can condensed milk
> 1 teaspoon vanilla extract
> 1 teaspoon pure orange flavoring, extract, or essence
> Pinch of salt

Caramelize the sugar according to the following directions.

While the sugar is caramelizing, heat the whole milk in a 3-quart saucepan and add the orange zest. Bring the milk just to a boil, turn off the heat, and let the zest steep in the milk until cool.

Preheat the oven to 350 degrees F and bring a quart of water to a boil.

Strain the milk into a clean bowl through a fine-mesh sieve and discard the zest.

Add the yolks and the whole egg to the milk and whisk until they are incorporated. Add the condensed milk and the vanilla, orange extract or essence, and salt. Whisk to blend, and then strain the milk mixture into the prepared pan. Follow the directions for cooking and serving the flan, baking it for 55–60 minutes.

CARAMELIZING THE SUGAR

Put $3/4$ cup sugar in a 10-inch skillet. Gently warm the sugar over medium heat until it melts and begins to turn brown. Watch it carefully toward the end so that it doesn't burn, but turns a rich, deep golden brown. Pour the melted sugar into an 8-inch cake pan, pie plate, or flan mold, tilting the pan so that the sugar runs around the bottom as evenly as possible. Don't fret if it isn't perfect.

COOKING THE FLAN

Set the filled flan pan into a larger pan. Carefully pour boiling water into the larger pan around the flan pan to a depth of an inch. Cook for the amount of time specified in the recipe. The flan is done when the surface looks set but the center of the flan still ripples slightly when jiggled. Gently remove the bain-marie pan and flan from the oven and let them cool to room temperature. The flan may be served at this point, but it will be firmer if it is refrigerated overnight.

SERVING THE FLAN

To serve, run a sharp knife around the side of the pan. Place a serving plate with a lip over the top of the pan and quickly invert the flan and the plate at the same time. The flan will drop onto the serving plate. Hold the plate absolutely horizontal so that the syrup doesn't run out! Cut in wedges and spoon a little syrup over each serving. Store any remaining flan in the refrigerator.

Pastel de Tres Leches

(Three-Milk Cake)

This is just one of the many versions of tres leches cake that can be found throughout Mexico and the United States. The simple, light sponge cake soaks up the three milks—dulce de leche or cajeta, milk, and whipping cream, making it moist and comforting.

Yields 10–12 slices

MILK MIXTURE

1 (13.5-ounce) can homemade dulce de leche*, or 1²/₃ cups purchased dulce de leche or cajeta (commercially made goat's milk caramel)

1 cup whole milk

1 cup whipping cream

1 teaspoon vanilla extract

1 tablespoon dark rum, optional

CAKE

4 tablespoons butter

1¹/₄ cups sifted cake flour

¹/₄ teaspoon salt

5 eggs, separated

³/₄ cup sugar, divided

2 teaspoons vanilla extract

1 teaspoon cream of tartar

1 cup cream

2 tablespoons confectioner's sugar

1 teaspoon vanilla

¹/₂ cup strawberry jam or cajeta, if desired, for filling

¹/₂ cup sweetened coconut, toasted

Sliced strawberries

For best results, pour the milk mixture over the cake as soon as it cools, and give it plenty of time to soak in. If you don't have time to make the dulce de leche and don't have a resource for the cajeta, use plain condensed milk.

Preheat oven to 350 degrees F. Cut out two circles of parchment paper to fit the bottom of two 8-inch cake pans. Butter and flour the pans.

Combine all ingredients for the milk mixture. Refrigerate.

For the cake, melt the butter and let it brown. Reserve. Combine the flour and the salt, whisk, and reserve. Beat egg yolks with ¹/₂ cup plus 2 tablespoons sugar and the vanilla until they are light colored and fluffy, 2–3 minutes. In a second bowl, beat the egg whites with the cream of tartar until soft peaks form. Sprinkle the remaining 2 tablespoons sugar over the whites with the beaters running and beat until they form stiff, glossy peaks.

Quickly stir ¹/₄ of the egg whites into the yolk mixture to lighten it. Sift ¹/₂ the flour mixture onto the yolks, and top with half the browned butter and half the remaining egg whites. Fold in gently, until it's partially mixed. Repeat with remaining flour, butter, and egg whites. Mix just until no streaks remain. (Don't overmix or the batter will deflate.)

Divide the batter between the prepared pans and smooth the tops. Place on the middle rack in the oven and bake for 20–25 minutes, or until the cakes are golden brown, the center is springy and bounces back, and the sides have pulled away from the pan.

Cool cakes completely on rack, then loosen sides by running a knife around the edge. One at a time, tip the cakes out of the pans onto a plate. Peel the parchment

Photo © 2009 Patricia Greathouse.

paper off the bottom and discard. Carefully put the cake back in the pan.

Puncture the cakes all over with a skewer, reaching all the way to the bottom. Slowly pour the milk mixture over the cake, focusing on the middle but letting it run down the sides, too. When the cake has absorbed the milk mixture, wrap well and refrigerate for several hours or overnight.

Whip the remaining cup cream with the confectioner's sugar and vanilla until it forms soft peaks. Reserve.

Put one of the cakes on a serving plate and spread 1/3 of the cream, cajeta, or jam over it. Carefully center the second cake on top of the first. Spread the remaining cream evenly over the top of the cake and garnish with toasted coconut or strawberries, if desired.

*DULCE DE LECHE

It's frightening to consider cooking canned goods in boiling water, much less cooking them in the pressure cooker. Although I haven't tried anything but condensed milk, I have done this many times with both of the methods that follow,

and nothing even mildly exciting has happened—except that I have made some delicious dulce de leche. (Some brands of condensed milk do have specific warnings not to cook unopened cans. Check the labels before proceeding.).

OPEN POT METHOD:

Remove the labels from cans of sweetened condensed milk. Put in a pot and fill with water to cover the cans by three inches. Bring to a boil and simmer for 3 hours. Let cool. Label the cans with a permanent marker before storing them.

PRESSURE COOKER METHOD:

Place a few cans of sweetened condensed milk in the pressure cooker and cover them with water. Bring to pressure and cook between 40 minutes and an hour. Let cool in the pressure cooker, or release pressure and cool.

Cans cooked for an hour and allowed to cool in the pressure cooker make very dark, thick dulce de leche. Stores on the shelf indefinitely.

Torta de Chocolate
(Mexican Chocolate Cake)

The flavors of Mexican hot chocolate in a light, moist, flourless cake. It can be made the day before serving and will still retain its soft, moist texture.

Yields 10–12 slices

1/3 cup raw whole almonds

3 whole tablets Mexican drinking chocolate (3.15 ounces each of La Abuelita, Mayordomo, or Ibarra brand), chopped

6 tablespoons unsalted butter, plus extra for cake pan

1/2 cup cream

1/4 cup Dutch process cocoa powder

1 teaspoon instant coffee

1/2 teaspoon cinnamon

1/8 teaspoon salt

2 teaspoons vanilla extract

1/2 teaspoon almond extract

4 room-temperature eggs, separated

6 tablespoons sugar, divided

1/2 teaspoon cream of tartar

Powdered sugar or cocoa, optional, for topping

Lightly sweetened whipped cream or crema for serving, optional

Preheat the oven to 325 degrees F. Line the bottom of an 8-inch spring-form pan with parchment paper and butter and flour the paper and sides of pan well.

Toast the almonds in the oven for eight minutes. Cool thoroughly. Grind in a food processor or nut grinder. Reserve.

Place the chocolate, butter, cream, cocoa, coffee, cinnamon, and salt in a double boiler. Melt chocolate, stirring often. Cool. Add the reserved ground almonds, vanilla, and almond extract to the chocolate mixture.

Beat the egg yolks and 4 tablespoons sugar together until light yellow and fluffy, 2–3 minutes. Fold the chocolate mixture into the egg yolks, scraping the bottom of the pan.

Beat the egg whites on medium-low speed until frothy, then add the cream of tartar and turn the speed up to high. Beat until the whites form soft peaks, then sprinkle on the remaining 2 tablespoons sugar with the beaters running. Beat until the whites are glossy and form stiff peaks. Mix 1/4 of the egg whites into the chocolate mixture to lighten it, and then fold in the rest of the whites with a few gentle strokes. There should be no visible streaks of white left.

Scrape the batter into the spring-form pan and smooth the top. Bake in the center of the preheated oven for 25 minutes, or until the cake has risen uniformly, is set around the edges, and still jiggles slightly in the center. Take care not to overbake.

Cool on a rack. After 15 minutes, run a sharp knife around the edge to loosen. (The cake will sink dramatically as it cools.) Remove the ring when completely cool. If desired, dust with sifted powdered sugar or cocoa right before serving. Garnish with soft, lightly sweetened whipped cream or crema.

Tequila

Tequila has become a huge industry in Mexico, largely because the margarita is the number-one mixed drink in the United States. Specialty margaritas come in options of gold or silver tequila, fresh-squeezed lemon or lime, and Curaçao or Grand Marnier. While cheap tequila was once known for fraternity party shooters, today high-quality tequila has become something to sip and savor for its complexity.

To presalt the cocktail glasses, put an even layer of coarse salt in a saucer. Run a piece of cut lime around the rim of the glass and put the glass rim down into the salt, then turn the glass upright and allow the salt to dry for at least 10 minutes. Turn the glass over and knock any loose salt out of the bottom before filling. Use a cocktail shaker or quart jar with tight-fitting lid for mixing the drink. Unless noted, the recipes below make one potent Margarita.

Photo © 2009 Christopher Barnes.

GOLD MARGARITA

2 ounces gold tequila
1 ounce Grand Marnier
Juice from 1/2 large, juicy lime
Lime wedge or wheel for garnish

SILVER MARGARITA

2 ounces silver tequila
1 ounce Cointreau
Juice from 1/2 large, juicy lime
Lime wedge or wheel for garnish

Fill cocktail shaker or jar with a tight-fitting lid full of clear ice. Add tequila, orange liqueur, and lime juice. Shake the mixture and then strain or pour with the ice into a salted glass; garnish with lime.

TAMARIND MARGARITA

The tamarind margarita is a specialty of the house at Casa Fuentes restaurant in Tlaquepaque, a cobblestoned artisanal village surrounded by the sprawl of Guadalajara.

1/2 teaspoon chile powder or flakes
1 lime, cut into quarters
1/2 teaspoon tamarind pulp
1 tablespoon simple syrup (see recipe that follows under Fruit Ices)
2 ounces silver tequila
1 ounce Grand Marnier
1/2 ounce freshly squeezed lime juice
1/2 ounce freshly squeezed orange juice
Ice

Put some coarse salt in a saucer and add the chile powder or flakes. Moisten the rim of a stemmed serving glass with a lime wedge and dip into the saucer, coating it with salt and chile. Reserve glass.

Put the rest of the ingredients except the ice into a blender and blend until there are no small pieces of tamarind visible. Add ice and blend briefly. Strain or pour into prepared glasses and garnish with a lime wedge.

Fruit Margaritas

Tequila connoisseurs might turn their noses up at these, but they're festive and summery, so put out a pitcher full for an outdoor party. Purists can sip their *reposada* (aged tequila) and sneer, but they'll be missing the fun!

STRAWBERRY MARGARITA

Beautiful, fresh, and fruity. Sugar the rim of the glass!

Makes about a quart

2 cups fresh ripe strawberries, stems removed
$1/4$ cup freshly squeezed lime juice
$1/2$ cup freshly squeezed orange juice
1 cup silver tequila
$1/2$ cup Cointreau
2 tablespoons Chambord

Put everything into the blender and blend until emulsified. Pour over ice and serve immediately, or chill for no more than a few hours, and shake well before pouring over ice.

MANGO-PEACH MARGARITA

Makes about a quart

$1^1/2$ cups peeled and seeded ripe mango
$1/2$ cup freshly squeezed lime juice
$1/2$ cup peach nectar
$3/4$ cup Grand Marnier
$1^1/2$ cups gold tequila

Follow directions above for the Strawberry Margarita.

BLUEBERRY MARGARITA

1 cup fresh blueberries, or substitute unthawed frozen berries
$1/4$ cup freshly squeezed lime juice
$1/2$ cup pomegranate tequila
$1/4$ cup Grand Marnier
$1/4$ cup agave nectar (as needed)

Follow directions above for the Strawberry Margarita.

CLASSIC MARGARITAS FOR A CROWD

This is a fantastic mix, tested scientifically by a number of guests. Make the margaritas no more than 2 to 3 hours in advance.

Makes a quart

1 cup freshly squeezed lime juice
2 cups gold tequila
$1/2$ cup Cointreau
$1/2$ cup Grand Marnier
Simple syrup to taste, if desired

Mix ingredients well. Chill. Shake or blend with ice, then pour or strain into salted glasses. Use lots of ice and blend to make frozen margaritas. Garnish with lime sections.

Fruit Ices

Refreshing and full of fresh, sprightly flavor, fruit ices are great served as dessert on a hot summer night and make a wonderful cocktail with a little tequila poured over them. The ices are simple to make and serve; guests can swirl the tequila around to mix it into the ice, or slowly sip the tequila while the ice melts.

To serve as a cocktail, scoop a tiny ball of fruit ice and pour a little tequila over it. Serve in a martini glass or champagne flute.

Master recipe instructions:

Any kind of commercial ice cream machine will work fine to make smooth ices. Alternately, freeze them in a shallow tray, scraping the ice crystals off the sides with a fork and mixing the ice every few hours. That will create a rougher, more crystallized ice. The ices keep well in the freezer, although after a few days they may separate. Whirl them in the food processor or whip with a balloon whisk and refreeze briefly before serving.

Basic simple syrup for ices:

> 4 cups sugar
> 2 cups water

TAMARIND ICE

Tamarind has a tart-sweet flavor that is a favorite of ours and is used to flavor Mexican sodas and candies.

> 1/2 cup tamarind pulp (available in Asian food stores and some supermarkets)
> 2 cups boiling water
> Simple syrup

Soak the tamarind in boiling water until it easily breaks up. Add simple syrup to taste. Strain through a sieve and freeze according to the master recipe.

PINK GRAPEFRUIT ICE

> 2 cups freshly squeezed Rio Star grapefruit juice, strained
> 1/2 cup simple syrup, or to taste

Mix the juice and simple syrup together and freeze according to the master recipe.

PINEAPPLE ICE

> 1 fresh pineapple
> 1/2 cup simple syrup, or to taste
> 2 cups water
> Juice of two limes, or to taste

Core and peel the pineapple, removing all the eyes. Cut in chunks and place in a food processor; grind to a purée. Put the pineapple in a nonreactive bowl and add the rest of the ingredients. It should be nicely balanced between sweet and tart. Freeze according to the master recipe.

REFERENCES

Bayless, Rick. *Mexico One Plate at a Time*. New York: Scribner, 2000.

Bayless, Rick and Deann Groen Bayless. *Authentic Mexican*. New York: William Morrow and Company, 1987.

Bayless, Rick. *Mexican Everyday*. New York: W. W. Norton, 2005.

Benítez, Ana M. de. *Pre-Hispanic Cooking*. Mexico, D.F.: Ediciones Euroamericanas Klaus Thiele, 1976.

Blanco, Jorge Ayala. *La Aventura del Cine Mexicano (en la Epoca de Oro y Despues)*. Mexico City: Editorial Grijalbo, S.A. de C.V., 1993.

Blankenship, Bill. "Pioneering Women Honored," *The Topeka Capital Journal* (July 18, 2006).

Buckley, Daniel. "Mariachi Revolution," *Tucson Citizen* (April 25, 2002).

Buraya, Luis Carlos. *Jorge Negrete*. Spain: Dastin, S.L., Ediciones y Distribuciones, Promo Libro, S.A. de C.V. España.

Burr, Ramiro. *The Billboard Guide to Tejano and Regional Mexican Music*. New York: Billboard Books, 1999.

Castillo, Jesús Amezcua. *Pedro Infante, Medio Siglo de Idolatría*. Mexico City: Ediciones B, S.A. de C. V. 2007.

Chavez, Denise. *Loving Pedro Infante*. New York: Washington Square Press, 2002.

Cope, R. Douglas. *The Limits of Racial Domination: Plebeian Society in Colonial Mexico City, 1660–1720*. Madison, WI: The University of Wisconsin Press, 1994.

Covarrubias, Antonio. "El Mariachi Suena," http: // members.tripod.com.

Denby, David. "Fallen Idols," *The New Yorker* (October 22, 2007), 108.

Escalante, Jesús Flores y. *Breve Historia de la Comida Mexicana*. Mexico, D. F.: Editorial Grijalbo, S. A. de C. V., 2003.

Evans, Tom and Mary Anne. *Guitars Music, History, Construction and Players*. New York: Oxford University Press, 1977.

Fogelquist, Mark Stephen. *Rhythm and Form in the Contemporary Son Jalisciense*. Los Angeles: University of California, 1975. Ph.D. Thesis.

Flores, Alejandro Flores T., ed. *Hombre y Mitos No. 27, Presenta: Pedro Infante*. Mexico, D.F.: Corporativo Mina, S.A. de C.V., 1998.

Garrido, Juan S. *Historia de la Música Popular en México: 1896–1973*. Mexico City: Editorial Extemporáneos, 1974.

Geijerstam, Claes af. *Popular Music in Mexico*. Albuquerque: University of New Mexico Press, 1976.

Gradante, William. "El Hijo del Pueblo": José Alfredo Jiménez and the Mexican "Canción Ranchera," *Latin American Music Review/Revista de Músic Latinoamericana* E (Spring-Summer 1982), 36–59.

Hoyer, Daniel. *Culinary Mexico*. Layton, Utah: Gibbs Smith, Publisher, 2005.

Jáuregui, Jésus. *El Mariachi, Símbolo Musical de Mexico*. Mexico, D.F.: Santillana Ediciones Generales, S.A. de C.V., 2007.

Jáuregui, Jésus. *La Plegaria Musical del Mariachi (Velada de Minuetes en la Catedral de Guadalajara)*. Mexico City: Instituto Nacional de Antropología e Historia, 1994.

Jáuregui, Jésus. *Los Mariachis de Mi Tierra . . . Noticias, Cuentos, Testimonios y Conjeturas: 1925–1994*. Mexico: Culturas Populares de Mexico, 1999.

Kennedy, Diana. *From My Mexican Kitchen*. New York: Clarkson Potter/Publisher, 2003.

Kennedy, Diana. *The Essential Cuisines of Mexico*. New York: Clarkson Potter/Publisher, 2000.

Kennedy, Diana. *My Mexico*. New York: Clarkson Potter/ Publisher, 1998.

López Domínguez, Ma. Emilia, "Nuestra Canción se Aprecia Más en el Extranjero," *La Música en México:*

Suplemento Mensual de El Dia 24 (July 1, 1974).

Lopez, Eric J. "Mariachi Music in the Public Schools: A Coping Strategy for Acculturating Students," Academic Exchange Extra (November 2004).

Mendez, Rodriguez Hermes Rafael. *Origen e Historia del Mariachi*. Mexico City: Editorial Katún, 1982.

Ortiz, Elizabeth Lambert. *The Complete Book of Mexican Cooking*. New York: M. Evans and Company, Inc. 1965.

Palomar, Cristina. "El Papel de la Charrería como Fenómeno Cultural en la Construcción del Occidente de México," *Revista Europea de Estudio Latino-americanos y del Caribe* 76 (April 2004), 83–98.

Parkes, Henry Bamford. *A History of Mexico*. 3rd ed. Boston: Houghton Mifflin Company, 1960.

Pérez, Leonor Xóchitl and Laura Sobrino. "The History of Women in Mariachi Music," http://www.sobrino.net/mpc/womenmariachi.

Poniatowska, Elena. "Consuelo Velazquez," *La Jornada* (July 20, 2003).

Prescott, William H. *History of the Conquest of Mexico*. New York: Modern Library, 2001.

Pulido, Marco Antonio, "Vida, Pasion, y Muerte de la Canción Mexicana." *Contenido* 79 (December 1969).

Purnell, Jenny. *Popular Movements and State Formation in Revolutionary Mexico: The Agraristas and Cristeros of Michoacán*. Durham, NC: Duke University Press, 1999.

Ramos, Samuel and Peter G. Earle (trans). *Profile of Man and Culture in Mexico*. Austin: University of Texas Press, 1962.

Riding, Alan. "Perpetual Mexican Fiesta," *New York Times* (July 4, 1982).

Rumbaut, Luis. "The Bolero," Latin American Folk Institute (Oct.–Dec. 2002), www.lafi.org/magazine/articles/bolero.html.

Sahagún, Fray Bernardino de. *Historia General de las Cosas de Nueva España 1*. Mexico City: Consejo Nacional Para la Cultura y Las Artes, 1989.

Schwartz, Stuart B. *Victors and Vanquished: Spanish and Nahua Views of the Conquest of Mexico*. Boston: Bedford/St. Martin's, 2000.

Sheehy, Daniel Edward. *Mariachi Music in America*. New York: Oxford University Press, 2006.

Sheehy, Daniel Edward. "Popular Mexican Musical Traditions: The Mariachi of West Mexico and the Conjunto Jaracho of Veracruz," in *Music in Latin American Culture: Regional Traditions,* ed. John M. Schechter Indianapolis: Schirmer Books. 1999, 34–78.

Simmons, Marc. *New Mexico: An Interpretive History*. Albuquerque: University of New Mexico Press, 1988.

Sonnichsen, Philip with Chris Strachwitz, ed. *The Earliest Mariachi Recordings*. El Cerrito, CA: Folklyric Records, 1986.

Torres, José Alejandro. *José Alfredo Jiménez*. México, D.F.: Grupo Editorial Tomo, S.A. de C.V., 2004.

Vásquez, Jorge Carrasco. *Pedro Infante*. Mexico, D.F.: Grupo Editorial Tomo, S.A. de C.V., 2005.

RESOURCES

MARIACHIS

Los Arrieros
    El Paso, TX
    915-592-1554
    http:// www.losarrieros.com

Mariachi Azteca
    Eddie Hernández, manager
    Santa Fe, New Mexico
    505-983-9196

Mariachi Colima
    Oakland, California
    510-533-4041
    http:// www.mariachicolima.com

Mariachi Chula Vista
    San Diego, California
    619-691-1611

Mariachi de América de Jesús
    Rodríguez de Híjar
    (011-52-555) 392-0759

Mariachi Divas
    http:www//mariachidivas.com

Mariachi Femenil Nuevo Tecalitlán
    Mariachi Nuevo Tecalitlán
    Guadalajara, Jalisco
    mariachi@mnt.com.mx

Mariachi Internacionál
    Guadalajara, Jalisco
    http:// www.mariachi-intguadalajara.com

Mariachi Los Toritos
    El Paso, Texas
    915-594-4626

Mariachi Mujer 2000
    http:www//mariachimujer2000.com

Mariachi Reyna de Los Angeles
    http://www.reynadelosangeles.com

Mariachi Sol de América
    Guadalajara, Jalisco
    33-36-56-46-33

Mariachi Sol de Mexico
    http://www.soldemexicoonline.com

Mariachi Son de México
    El Paso, Texas
    915-346-7953

Mariachi Tenampa
    Albuquerque, New Mexico
    http:// www.mariachitenampa.net

Mariachi Vargas de Tecalitlán
    http:www//mariachivargas.net

CHARRO CLOTHING AND MARIACHI MUSIC

El Charro (boots, trajes de charros, hats)
    El Paso, Texas
    http:www//elcharro1.com
    1-877-980-1248

J.G. Ara (wide selection of handcrafted earrings for mariachi women)
    San Antonio, Texas
    210-680-9809

Jorge Nuñez (tailor— trajes de charros)
    Juarez # 36 Col. Centro
    Guadalajara, Jalisco
    (33) 3613-7754

Juan Mercado S. (musical instruments, photos, CDs, and accessories)
    (0155) 55295099 55 26 01 76
    Plaza Garibaldi, Mexico City
    Contactogaribaldi@hotmail.com

MABO (boots, belts, hats)
    3657-4598
    Tlaquepaque, Jalisco

Sastreria Jalisco (tailor—trajes de charros)
    Eduardo Garcia E.
    (656) 612 –2109
    Juárez, Mexico

Sombreros Castillo
    Mercado Libertad local no. 101
    (0133) 3618-65-88
    Guadalajara, Jalisco

The Mariachi Connection, Inc.
    http:// www.mariachiconnection.com

MEXICAN GROCERIES, CHILES, AND SPICES:

http:// www.gourmetsleuth.com/chocolatemayordomo.htm

http:// www.leosimports.com

http:// www.mexgrocer.com

http:// www. newmexicanconnection.com

http:// www.penzeys.com
(excellent quality chiles)

MISCELLANEOUS

Silvestre Vargas Museum (site for tourist references—good handicrafts and art)
    http://www.fiestaweb.org/Biographies/VargasE.cfm

Tecalitlán
    http://www.tecalitlan.gob.mx/turismo.php

Tequila Express
    Guadalajara, Jalisco
    http://www.tequilaexpress.com.mx

GREAT WEB SITES

http://www.elmariachi.com/

http://www.fiestaweb.org/

http://www.mariachi.org/

http://www.mariachi-publishing.com/

http://www.mariachi4u.com

http://www.menc.org/mariachi

http://www.mexicanmercados.com

INDEX

METRIC CONVERSION CHART

LIQUID AND DRY MEASURES

U.S.	Canadian	Australian
¼ teaspoon	1 mL	1 ml
½ teaspoon	2 mL	2 ml
1 teaspoon	5 mL	5 ml
1 tablespoon	15 mL	20 ml
¼ cup	50 mL	60 ml
⅓ cup	75 mL	80 ml
½ cup	125 mL	125 ml
⅔ cup	150 mL	170 ml
¾ cup	175 mL	190 ml
1 cup	250 mL	250 ml
1 quart	1 liter	1 litre

TEMPERATURE CONVERSION CHART

Fahrenheit	Celsius
250	120
275	140
300	150
325	160
350	180
375	190
400	200
425	220
450	230
475	240
500	260

PAGE · KATY JURADO

ALAJARA
PUES

JALISCO
NUNCA PIERDE

ORES CAMARILLO · RAUL HERNANDEZ · JOSE LUIS SALGADO
RO DE URDIMALAS, ALFREDO GUTIERREZ · MARIO GARCIA 'MANO'
Actuación especial de AUGUSTO BENEDICO
GILBERTO PARRA · RAUL DOMINGUEZ
Dirección de RENE CARDONA.

RA CUAL.

CINEMATOGRAFICA FILMEX, S. A. presenta a:

ANTONIO AGUILAR
FLOR SILVESTRE · JAIME FERNANDEZ en

EPISODIOS:
"LA TUMBA ABANDONADA"
"EL ESPIA DE VILLA"
"LA MUERTE DE PANCHO VILLA"

CABALLO
PRIETO
AZABACHE
(LA TUMBA DE VILLA)

a COLORES

ARGUMENTO Y CINEDRAMA: RAFAEL GARCIA TRAVESI
MUSICA: ENRICO CABIATI · FOTOGRAFIA: FERNANDO COLIN
DIRECCION y
GUION TECNICO: **RENE CARDONA**

CON JORGE RUSSEK · JESSICA MUNGUIA · GUILLERMO RIVAS
Y LA PRESENTACION DE
TITO NOVARO · JOSE LUIS MORENO · ALEJANDRO REYNA (Tio PLACIDO)

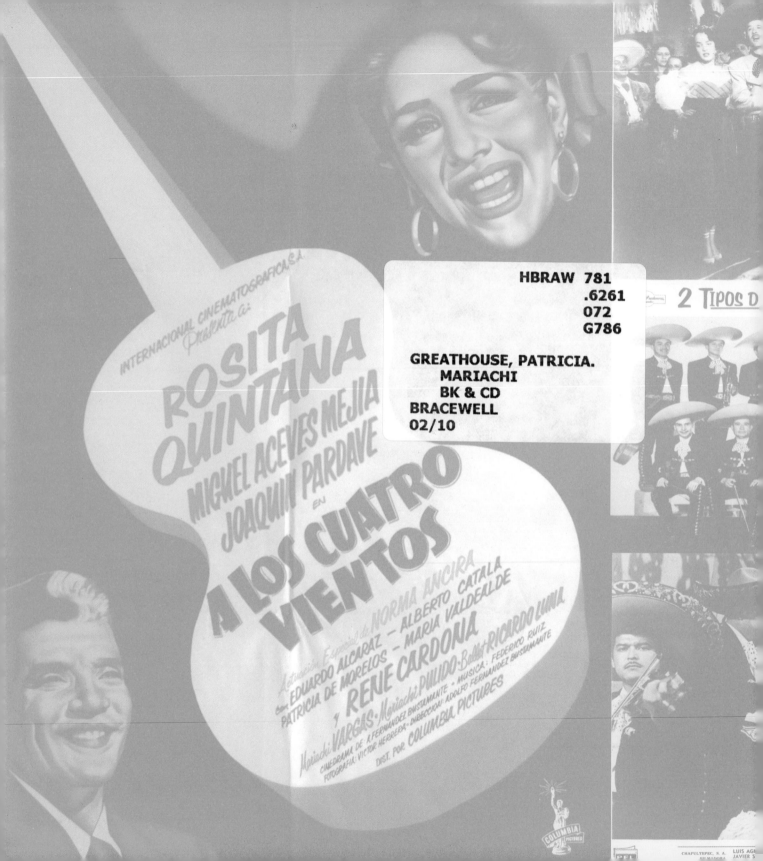